# How to Mak

## A Handbook for Teens, Kids & Young Adults

# HOW TO USE THIS BOOK:

Color one or two pictures everyday.
Think about the job that each person is doing.
Could it be you?

## TO DISCOVER HOW TO START EARNING MONEY ANSWER THESE "THINKING QUESTIONS" ABOUT EACH PICTURE:

1. What is this profession called?
2. What would the world be like if no one did this job?
3. What is a person with this profession expected to accomplish?
4. Could you be good at this job? Why?
5. What kind of education, ability, training and experience does a person need to do this job well?
6. How much money can a person earn when they do this job as a full time profession?
7. How much time does this job require?
8. Do you know someone with this job?
9. On a scale from one to ten, rate this job.
10. What is the best thing about this job, and the worst thing about this job?

# ACTION STEPS:

1. Make a list of the TOP TEN Jobs that interest you.

2. Learn everything you can about those ten jobs.
Read books, watch videos and talk to people who do the jobs that interest you.

3. When you learn everything you can about those jobs, narrow your list down to four occupations that you might pursue.

4. Interview people with those four jobs.

5. Train yourself to become an expert about your TWO favorite occupations.

6. Volunteer or intern as an assistant to someone with your favorite job.

7. Acquire the education, experience, abilities and skills to be the best at this profession.

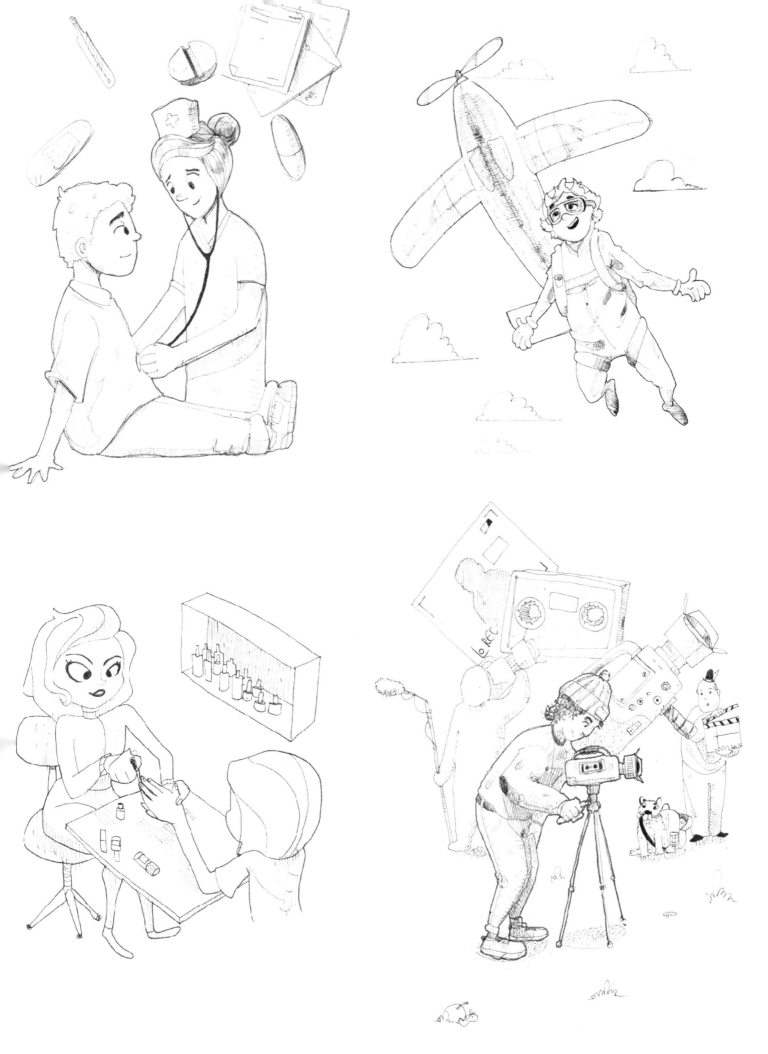

# PLANS AND GOALS

What do you want to be doing two years from now? YEAR:
_____ My Age:_____

_____

_____

_____

_____

What do you want to be doing 15 years from now?
YEAR:_____ My Age:_____

_____

_____

_____

_____

_____

What do your need to LEARN or CHANGE in your life now so you can reach your future goals?

_____

_____

_____

_____

_____

_____

# THINKING QUESTIONS

1. What is this profession called?

   _____

   _____

2. What would the world be like if no one did this job?

   _____

   _____

   _____

3. What is a person with this job expected to accomplish?

   _____

   _____

   _____

4. Could you be good at this job? _____ Why?

   _____

   _____

   _____

5. What kind of education, ability, training and experience does a person need to do this job well?

   _____

   _____

   _____

6. How much money can a person earn when they do this job as a profession?

   _____

7. How much time does this job require?

   _____

8. Do you know someone with this job?

   _____

9. On a scale from one to ten, rate this job. 1 2 3 4 5 6 7 8 9 10

10. What is the best thing about this job and the worst thing about this job?

    _____

    _____

    _____

    _____

    _____

# THINKING QUESTIONS

1. What is this profession called?

   ------------------------------------------------

   ------------------------------------------------

2. What would the world be like if no one did this job?

   ------------------------------------------------

   ------------------------------------------------

   ------------------------------------------------

3. What is a person with this job expected to accomplish?

   ------------------------------------------------

   ------------------------------------------------

   ------------------------------------------------

4. Could you be good at this job? _____ Why?

   ------------------------------------------------

   ------------------------------------------------

   ------------------------------------------------

5. What kind of education, ability, training and experience does a person need to do this job well?

   ------------------------------------------------

   ------------------------------------------------

   ------------------------------------------------

6. How much money can a person earn when they do this job as a profession?

   ------------------------------------------------

7. How much time does this job require?

   ------------------------------------------------

8. Do you know someone with this job?

   ------------------------------------------------

9. On a scale from one to ten, rate this job. 1 2 3 4 5 6 7 8 9 10

10. What is the best thing about this job and the worst thing about this job?

    ------------------------------------------------

    ------------------------------------------------

    ------------------------------------------------

    ------------------------------------------------

    ------------------------------------------------

    ------------------------------------------------

# THINKING QUESTIONS

1. What is this profession called?

   ------------------------------------------

   ------------------------------------------

2. What would the world be like if no one did this job?

   ------------------------------------------

   ------------------------------------------

   ------------------------------------------

3. What is a person with this job expected to accomplish?

   ------------------------------------------

   ------------------------------------------

   ------------------------------------------

4. Could you be good at this job? _____ Why?

   ------------------------------------------

   ------------------------------------------

   ------------------------------------------

5. What kind of education, ability, training and experience does a person need to do this job well?

   ------------------------------------------

   ------------------------------------------

   ------------------------------------------

6. How much money can a person earn when they do this job as a profession?

   ------------------------------------------

7. How much time does this job require?

   ------------------------------------------

8. Do you know someone with this job?

   ------------------------------------------

9. On a scale from one to ten, rate this job. 1 2 3 4 5 6 7 8 9 10

10. What is the best thing about this job and the worst thing about this job?

    ------------------------------------------

    ------------------------------------------

    ------------------------------------------

    ------------------------------------------

    ------------------------------------------

    ------------------------------------------

# THINKING QUESTIONS

1. What is this profession called?

   ---------------------------------------------------------------

   ---------------------------------------------------------------

2. What would the world be like if no one did this job?

   ---------------------------------------------------------------

   ---------------------------------------------------------------

   ---------------------------------------------------------------

3. What is a person with this job expected to accomplish?

   ---------------------------------------------------------------

   ---------------------------------------------------------------

   ---------------------------------------------------------------

4. Could you be good at this job? _____ Why?

   ---------------------------------------------------------------

   ---------------------------------------------------------------

   ---------------------------------------------------------------

5. What kind of education, ability, training and experience does a person need to do this job well?

   ---------------------------------------------------------------

   ---------------------------------------------------------------

   ---------------------------------------------------------------

6. How much money can a person earn when they do this job as a profession?

   ---------------------------------------------------------------

7. How much time does this job require?

   ---------------------------------------------------------------

8. Do you know someone with this job?

   ---------------------------------------------------------------

9. On a scale from one to ten, rate this job. 1 2 3 4 5 6 7 8 9 10

10. What is the best thing about this job and the worst thing about this job?

    ---------------------------------------------------------------

    ---------------------------------------------------------------

    ---------------------------------------------------------------

    ---------------------------------------------------------------

    ---------------------------------------------------------------

    ---------------------------------------------------------------

# THINKING QUESTIONS

1. What is this profession called?

   -------------------------------------------------------------

   -------------------------------------------------------------

2. What would the world be like if no one did this job?

   -------------------------------------------------------------

   -------------------------------------------------------------

   -------------------------------------------------------------

3. What is a person with this job expected to accomplish?

   -------------------------------------------------------------

   -------------------------------------------------------------

   -------------------------------------------------------------

4. Could you be good at this job? _____ Why?

   -------------------------------------------------------------

   -------------------------------------------------------------

   -------------------------------------------------------------

5. What kind of education, ability, training and experience does a person need to do this job well?

   -------------------------------------------------------------

   -------------------------------------------------------------

   -------------------------------------------------------------

6. How much money can a person earn when they do this job as a profession?

   -------------------------------------------------------------

7. How much time does this job require?

   -------------------------------------------------------------

8. Do you know someone with this job?

   -------------------------------------------------------------

9. On a scale from one to ten, rate this job. 1 2 3 4 5 6 7 8 9 10

10. What is the best thing about this job and the worst thing about this job?

    -------------------------------------------------------------

    -------------------------------------------------------------

    -------------------------------------------------------------

    -------------------------------------------------------------

    -------------------------------------------------------------

    -------------------------------------------------------------

# THINKING QUESTIONS

1. What is this profession called?

   ------------------------------------------------

   ------------------------------------------------

2. What would the world be like if no one did this job?

   ------------------------------------------------

   ------------------------------------------------

   ------------------------------------------------

3. What is a person with this job expected to accomplish?

   ------------------------------------------------

   ------------------------------------------------

   ------------------------------------------------

4. Could you be good at this job? _____ Why?

   ------------------------------------------------

   ------------------------------------------------

   ------------------------------------------------

5. What kind of education, ability, training and experience does a person need to do this job well?

   ------------------------------------------------

   ------------------------------------------------

   ------------------------------------------------

6. How much money can a person earn when they do this job as a profession?

   ------------------------------------------------

7. How much time does this job require?

   ------------------------------------------------

8. Do you know someone with this job?

   ------------------------------------------------

9. On a scale from one to ten, rate this job. 1 2 3 4 5 6 7 8 9 10

10. What is the best thing about this job and the worst thing about this job?

   ------------------------------------------------

   ------------------------------------------------

   ------------------------------------------------

   ------------------------------------------------

   ------------------------------------------------

   ------------------------------------------------

# THINKING QUESTIONS

1. What is this profession called?

   ------------------------------------------------

   ------------------------------------------------

2. What would the world be like if no one did this job?

   ------------------------------------------------

   ------------------------------------------------

   ------------------------------------------------

3. What is a person with this job expected to accomplish?

   ------------------------------------------------

   ------------------------------------------------

   ------------------------------------------------

4. Could you be good at this job? _____ Why?

   ------------------------------------------------

   ------------------------------------------------

   ------------------------------------------------

5. What kind of education, ability, training and experience does a person need to do this job well?

   ------------------------------------------------

   ------------------------------------------------

   ------------------------------------------------

6. How much money can a person earn when they do this job as a profession?

   ------------------------------------------------

7. How much time does this job require?

   ------------------------------------------------

8. Do you know someone with this job?

   ------------------------------------------------

9. On a scale from one to ten, rate this job. 1 2 3 4 5 6 7 8 9 10
10. What is the best thing about this job and the worst thing about this job?

   ------------------------------------------------

   ------------------------------------------------

   ------------------------------------------------

   ------------------------------------------------

   ------------------------------------------------

   ------------------------------------------------

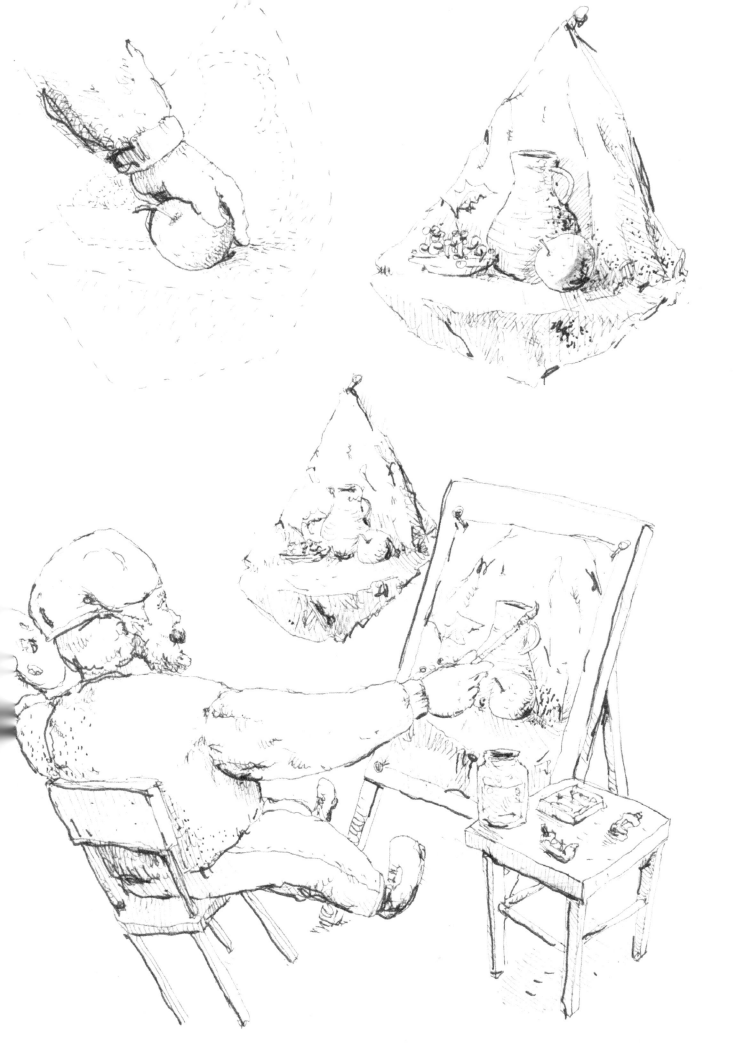

# THINKING QUESTIONS

1. What is this profession called?

   ------------------------------------------------

   ------------------------------------------------

2. What would the world be like if no one did this job?

   ------------------------------------------------

   ------------------------------------------------

   ------------------------------------------------

3. What is a person with this job expected to accomplish?

   ------------------------------------------------

   ------------------------------------------------

   ------------------------------------------------

4. Could you be good at this job? _____ Why?

   ------------------------------------------------

   ------------------------------------------------

   ------------------------------------------------

5. What kind of education, ability, training and experience does a person need to do this job well?

   ------------------------------------------------

   ------------------------------------------------

   ------------------------------------------------

6. How much money can a person earn when they do this job as a profession?

   ------------------------------------------------

7. How much time does this job require?

   ------------------------------------------------

8. Do you know someone with this job?

   ------------------------------------------------

9. On a scale from one to ten, rate this job. 1 2 3 4 5 6 7 8 9 10

10. What is the best thing about this job and the worst thing about this job?

    ------------------------------------------------

    ------------------------------------------------

    ------------------------------------------------

    ------------------------------------------------

    ------------------------------------------------

    ------------------------------------------------

# THINKING QUESTIONS

1. What is this profession called?

   _____

   _____

2. What would the world be like if no one did this job?

   _____

   _____

   _____

3. What is a person with this job expected to accomplish?

   _____

   _____

   _____

4. Could you be good at this job? _____ Why?

   _____

   _____

   _____

5. What kind of education, ability, training and experience does a person need to do this job well?

   _____

   _____

   _____

6. How much money can a person earn when they do this job as a profession?

   _____

7. How much time does this job require?

   _____

8. Do you know someone with this job?

   _____

9. On a scale from one to ten, rate this job. 1 2 3 4 5 6 7 8 9 10

10. What is the best thing about this job and the worst thing about this job?

    _____

    _____

    _____

    _____

    _____

# THINKING QUESTIONS

1. What is this profession called?

   _____

   _____

2. What would the world be like if no one did this job?

   _____

   _____

   _____

3. What is a person with this job expected to accomplish?

   _____

   _____

   _____

4. Could you be good at this job? _____ Why?

   _____

   _____

   _____

5. What kind of education, ability, training and experience does a person need to do this job well?

   _____

   _____

   _____

6. How much money can a person earn when they do this job as a profession?

   _____

7. How much time does this job require?

   _____

8. Do you know someone with this job?

   _____

9. On a scale from one to ten, rate this job. 1 2 3 4 5 6 7 8 9 10

10. What is the best thing about this job and the worst thing about this job?

   _____

   _____

   _____

   _____

   _____

# THINKING QUESTIONS

1. What is this profession called?

   ------------------------------------------------

   ------------------------------------------------

2. What would the world be like if no one did this job?

   ------------------------------------------------

   ------------------------------------------------

   ------------------------------------------------

3. What is a person with this job expected to accomplish?

   ------------------------------------------------

   ------------------------------------------------

   ------------------------------------------------

4. Could you be good at this job? _____ Why?

   ------------------------------------------------

   ------------------------------------------------

   ------------------------------------------------

5. What kind of education, ability, training and experience does a person need to do this job well?

   ------------------------------------------------

   ------------------------------------------------

   ------------------------------------------------

6. How much money can a person earn when they do this job as a profession?

   ------------------------------------------------

7. How much time does this job require?

   ------------------------------------------------

8. Do you know someone with this job?

   ------------------------------------------------

9. On a scale from one to ten, rate this job. 1 2 3 4 5 6 7 8 9 10

10. What is the best thing about this job and the worst thing about this job?

    ------------------------------------------------

    ------------------------------------------------

    ------------------------------------------------

    ------------------------------------------------

    ------------------------------------------------

    ------------------------------------------------

# THINKING QUESTIONS

1.  What is this profession called?

    ------------------------------------------------------------

    ------------------------------------------------------------

2.  What would the world be like if no one did this job?

    ------------------------------------------------------------

    ------------------------------------------------------------

    ------------------------------------------------------------

3.  What is a person with this job expected to accomplish?

    ------------------------------------------------------------

    ------------------------------------------------------------

    ------------------------------------------------------------

4.  Could you be good at this job? _____ Why?

    ------------------------------------------------------------

    ------------------------------------------------------------

    ------------------------------------------------------------

5.  What kind of education, ability, training and experience does a person need to do this job well?

    ------------------------------------------------------------

    ------------------------------------------------------------

    ------------------------------------------------------------

6.  How much money can a person earn when they do this job as a profession?

    ------------------------------------------------------------

7.  How much time does this job require?

    ------------------------------------------------------------

8.  Do you know someone with this job?

    ------------------------------------------------------------

9.  On a scale from one to ten, rate this job. 1 2 3 4 5 6 7 8 9 10

10. What is the best thing about this job and the worst thing about this job?

    ------------------------------------------------------------

    ------------------------------------------------------------

    ------------------------------------------------------------

    ------------------------------------------------------------

    ------------------------------------------------------------

# THINKING QUESTIONS

1.  What is this profession called?

    ----------------------------------------------------------------

    ----------------------------------------------------------------

2.  What would the world be like if no one did this job?

    ----------------------------------------------------------------

    ----------------------------------------------------------------

    ----------------------------------------------------------------

3.  What is a person with this job expected to accomplish?

    ----------------------------------------------------------------

    ----------------------------------------------------------------

    ----------------------------------------------------------------

4.  Could you be good at this job? _____ Why?

    ----------------------------------------------------------------

    ----------------------------------------------------------------

    ----------------------------------------------------------------

5.  What kind of education, ability, training and experience does a person need to do this job well?

    ----------------------------------------------------------------

    ----------------------------------------------------------------

    ----------------------------------------------------------------

6.  How much money can a person earn when they do this job as a profession?

    ----------------------------------------------------------------

7.  How much time does this job require?

    ----------------------------------------------------------------

8.  Do you know someone with this job?

    ----------------------------------------------------------------

9.  On a scale from one to ten, rate this job. 1 2 3 4 5 6 7 8 9 10

10. What is the best thing about this job and the worst thing about this job?

    ----------------------------------------------------------------

    ----------------------------------------------------------------

    ----------------------------------------------------------------

    ----------------------------------------------------------------

    ----------------------------------------------------------------

    ----------------------------------------------------------------

# THINKING QUESTIONS

1. What is this profession called?

   ------------------------------------------------------------

   ------------------------------------------------------------

2. What would the world be like if no one did this job?

   ------------------------------------------------------------

   ------------------------------------------------------------

   ------------------------------------------------------------

3. What is a person with this job expected to accomplish?

   ------------------------------------------------------------

   ------------------------------------------------------------

   ------------------------------------------------------------

4. Could you be good at this job? _____ Why?

   ------------------------------------------------------------

   ------------------------------------------------------------

   ------------------------------------------------------------

5. What kind of education, ability, training and experience does a person need to do this job well?

   ------------------------------------------------------------

   ------------------------------------------------------------

   ------------------------------------------------------------

6. How much money can a person earn when they do this job as a profession?

   ------------------------------------------------------------

7. How much time does this job require?

   ------------------------------------------------------------

8. Do you know someone with this job?

   ------------------------------------------------------------

9. On a scale from one to ten, rate this job. 1 2 3 4 5 6 7 8 9 10

10. What is the best thing about this job and the worst thing about this job?

    ------------------------------------------------------------

    ------------------------------------------------------------

    ------------------------------------------------------------

    ------------------------------------------------------------

    ------------------------------------------------------------

    ------------------------------------------------------------

# THINKING QUESTIONS

1. What is this profession called?

   ------------------------------------------------------------

   ------------------------------------------------------------

2. What would the world be like if no one did this job?

   ------------------------------------------------------------

   ------------------------------------------------------------

   ------------------------------------------------------------

3. What is a person with this job expected to accomplish?

   ------------------------------------------------------------

   ------------------------------------------------------------

   ------------------------------------------------------------

4. Could you be good at this job? _____ Why?

   ------------------------------------------------------------

   ------------------------------------------------------------

   ------------------------------------------------------------

5. What kind of education, ability, training and experience does a person need to do this job well?

   ------------------------------------------------------------

   ------------------------------------------------------------

   ------------------------------------------------------------

6. How much money can a person earn when they do this job as a profession?

   ------------------------------------------------------------

7. How much time does this job require?

   ------------------------------------------------------------

8. Do you know someone with this job?

   ------------------------------------------------------------

9. On a scale from one to ten, rate this job. 1 2 3 4 5 6 7 8 9 10

10. What is the best thing about this job and the worst thing about this job?

   ------------------------------------------------------------

   ------------------------------------------------------------

   ------------------------------------------------------------

   ------------------------------------------------------------

   ------------------------------------------------------------

   ------------------------------------------------------------

# THINKING QUESTIONS

1.  What is this profession called?

    ----------------------------------------------------------------
    ----------------------------------------------------------------

2.  What would the world be like if no one did this job?

    ----------------------------------------------------------------
    ----------------------------------------------------------------
    ----------------------------------------------------------------

3.  What is a person with this job expected to accomplish?

    ----------------------------------------------------------------
    ----------------------------------------------------------------
    ----------------------------------------------------------------

4.  Could you be good at this job? _____ Why?

    ----------------------------------------------------------------
    ----------------------------------------------------------------
    ----------------------------------------------------------------

5.  What kind of education, ability, training and experience does a person need to do this job well?

    ----------------------------------------------------------------
    ----------------------------------------------------------------
    ----------------------------------------------------------------

6.  How much money can a person earn when they do this job as a profession?

    ----------------------------------------------------------------

7.  How much time does this job require?

    ----------------------------------------------------------------

8.  Do you know someone with this job?

    ----------------------------------------------------------------

9.  On a scale from one to ten, rate this job. 1 2 3 4 5 6 7 8 9 10

10. What is the best thing about this job and the worst thing about this job?

    ----------------------------------------------------------------
    ----------------------------------------------------------------
    ----------------------------------------------------------------
    ----------------------------------------------------------------
    ----------------------------------------------------------------
    ----------------------------------------------------------------

# THINKING QUESTIONS

1. What is this profession called?

   ---------------------------------------------------------

   ---------------------------------------------------------

2. What would the world be like if no one did this job?

   ---------------------------------------------------------

   ---------------------------------------------------------

   ---------------------------------------------------------

3. What is a person with this job expected to accomplish?

   ---------------------------------------------------------

   ---------------------------------------------------------

   ---------------------------------------------------------

4. Could you be good at this job? _____ Why?

   ---------------------------------------------------------

   ---------------------------------------------------------

   ---------------------------------------------------------

5. What kind of education, ability, training and experience does a person need to do this job well?

   ---------------------------------------------------------

   ---------------------------------------------------------

   ---------------------------------------------------------

6. How much money can a person earn when they do this job as a profession?

   ---------------------------------------------------------

7. How much time does this job require?

   ---------------------------------------------------------

8. Do you know someone with this job?

   ---------------------------------------------------------

9. On a scale from one to ten, rate this job. 1 2 3 4 5 6 7 8 9 10

10. What is the best thing about this job and the worst thing about this job?

    ---------------------------------------------------------

    ---------------------------------------------------------

    ---------------------------------------------------------

    ---------------------------------------------------------

    ---------------------------------------------------------

    ---------------------------------------------------------

# THINKING QUESTIONS

1. What is this profession called?

   ------------------------------------------------------------

   ------------------------------------------------------------

2. What would the world be like if no one did this job?

   ------------------------------------------------------------

   ------------------------------------------------------------

   ------------------------------------------------------------

3. What is a person with this job expected to accomplish?

   ------------------------------------------------------------

   ------------------------------------------------------------

   ------------------------------------------------------------

4. Could you be good at this job? _____ Why?

   ------------------------------------------------------------

   ------------------------------------------------------------

   ------------------------------------------------------------

5. What kind of education, ability, training and experience does a person need to do this job well?

   ------------------------------------------------------------

   ------------------------------------------------------------

   ------------------------------------------------------------

6. How much money can a person earn when they do this job as a profession?

   ------------------------------------------------------------

7. How much time does this job require?

   ------------------------------------------------------------

8. Do you know someone with this job?

   ------------------------------------------------------------

9. On a scale from one to ten, rate this job. 1 2 3 4 5 6 7 8 9 10

10. What is the best thing about this job and the worst thing about this job?

    ------------------------------------------------------------

    ------------------------------------------------------------

    ------------------------------------------------------------

    ------------------------------------------------------------

    ------------------------------------------------------------

    ------------------------------------------------------------

# THINKING QUESTIONS

1. What is this profession called?

   --------------------------------------------------------------

   --------------------------------------------------------------

2. What would the world be like if no one did this job?

   --------------------------------------------------------------

   --------------------------------------------------------------

   --------------------------------------------------------------

3. What is a person with this job expected to accomplish?

   --------------------------------------------------------------

   --------------------------------------------------------------

   --------------------------------------------------------------

4. Could you be good at this job? _____ Why?

   --------------------------------------------------------------

   --------------------------------------------------------------

   --------------------------------------------------------------

5. What kind of education, ability, training and experience does a person need to do this job well?

   --------------------------------------------------------------

   --------------------------------------------------------------

   --------------------------------------------------------------

6. How much money can a person earn when they do this job as a profession?

   --------------------------------------------------------------

7. How much time does this job require?

   --------------------------------------------------------------

8. Do you know someone with this job?

   --------------------------------------------------------------

9. On a scale from one to ten, rate this job. 1 2 3 4 5 6 7 8 9 10

10. What is the best thing about this job and the worst thing about this job?

   --------------------------------------------------------------

   --------------------------------------------------------------

   --------------------------------------------------------------

   --------------------------------------------------------------

   --------------------------------------------------------------

   --------------------------------------------------------------

# THINKING QUESTIONS

1.  What is this profession called?

    ----------------------------------------------------------------
    ----------------------------------------------------------------

2.  What would the world be like if no one did this job?

    ----------------------------------------------------------------
    ----------------------------------------------------------------
    ----------------------------------------------------------------

3.  What is a person with this job expected to accomplish?

    ----------------------------------------------------------------
    ----------------------------------------------------------------
    ----------------------------------------------------------------

4.  Could you be good at this job? _____ Why?

    ----------------------------------------------------------------
    ----------------------------------------------------------------
    ----------------------------------------------------------------

5.  What kind of education, ability, training and experience does a person need to do this job well?

    ----------------------------------------------------------------
    ----------------------------------------------------------------
    ----------------------------------------------------------------

6.  How much money can a person earn when they do this job as a profession?

    ----------------------------------------------------------------

7.  How much time does this job require?

    ----------------------------------------------------------------

8.  Do you know someone with this job?

    ----------------------------------------------------------------

9.  On a scale from one to ten, rate this job. 1 2 3 4 5 6 7 8 9 10

10. What is the best thing about this job and the worst thing about this job?

    ----------------------------------------------------------------
    ----------------------------------------------------------------
    ----------------------------------------------------------------
    ----------------------------------------------------------------
    ----------------------------------------------------------------
    ----------------------------------------------------------------

# THINKING QUESTIONS

1. What is this profession called?

   ------------------------------------------------------------

   ------------------------------------------------------------

2. What would the world be like if no one did this job?

   ------------------------------------------------------------

   ------------------------------------------------------------

   ------------------------------------------------------------

3. What is a person with this job expected to accomplish?

   ------------------------------------------------------------

   ------------------------------------------------------------

   ------------------------------------------------------------

4. Could you be good at this job? _____ Why?

   ------------------------------------------------------------

   ------------------------------------------------------------

   ------------------------------------------------------------

5. What kind of education, ability, training and experience does a person need to do this job well?

   ------------------------------------------------------------

   ------------------------------------------------------------

   ------------------------------------------------------------

6. How much money can a person earn when they do this job as a profession?

   ------------------------------------------------------------

7. How much time does this job require?

   ------------------------------------------------------------

8. Do you know someone with this job?

   ------------------------------------------------------------

9. On a scale from one to ten, rate this job. 1 2 3 4 5 6 7 8 9 10
10. What is the best thing about this job and the worst thing about this job?

    ------------------------------------------------------------

    ------------------------------------------------------------

    ------------------------------------------------------------

    ------------------------------------------------------------

    ------------------------------------------------------------

    ------------------------------------------------------------

# THINKING QUESTIONS

1. What is this profession called?

   _____

   _____

2. What would the world be like if no one did this job?

   _____

   _____

   _____

3. What is a person with this job expected to accomplish?

   _____

   _____

   _____

4. Could you be good at this job? _____ Why?

   _____

   _____

   _____

5. What kind of education, ability, training and experience does a person need to do this job well?

   _____

   _____

   _____

6. How much money can a person earn when they do this job as a profession?

   _____

7. How much time does this job require?

   _____

8. Do you know someone with this job?

   _____

9. On a scale from one to ten, rate this job. 1 2 3 4 5 6 7 8 9 10

10. What is the best thing about this job and the worst thing about this job?

    _____

    _____

    _____

    _____

    _____

    _____

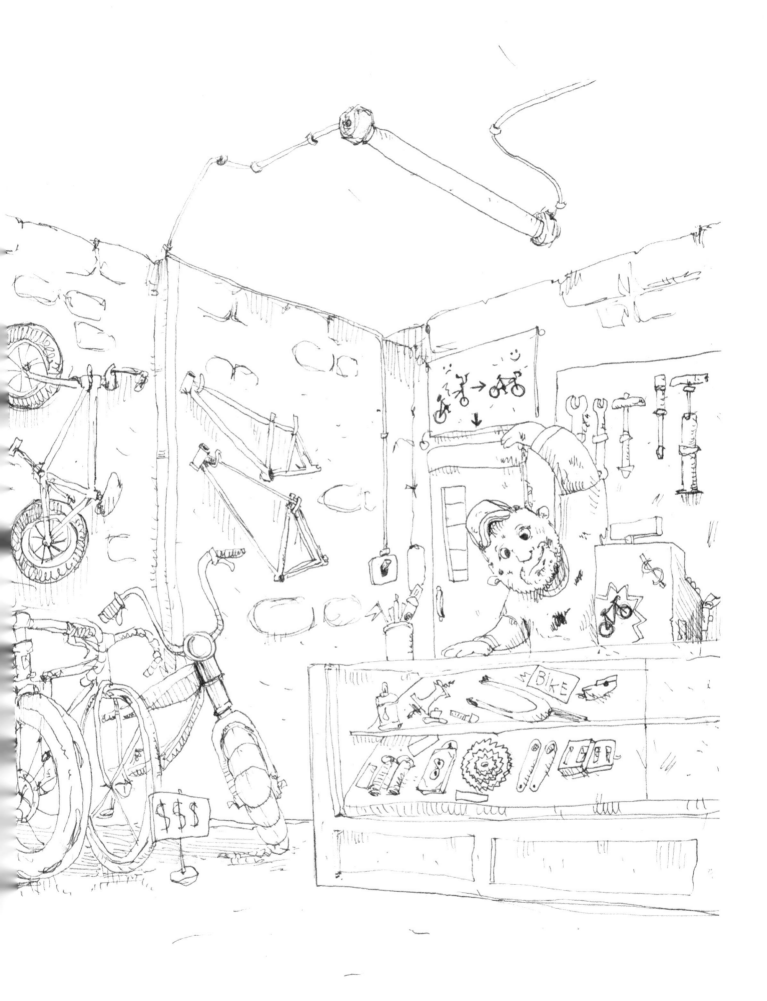

# THINKING QUESTIONS

1. What is this profession called?

   _____

   _____

2. What would the world be like if no one did this job?

   _____

   _____

   _____

3. What is a person with this job expected to accomplish?

   _____

   _____

   _____

4. Could you be good at this job? _____ Why?

   _____

   _____

   _____

5. What kind of education, ability, training and experience does a person need to do this job well?

   _____

   _____

   _____

6. How much money can a person earn when they do this job as a profession?

   _____

7. How much time does this job require?

   _____

8. Do you know someone with this job?

   _____

9. On a scale from one to ten, rate this job. 1 2 3 4 5 6 7 8 9 10
10. What is the best thing about this job and the worst thing about this job?

   _____

   _____

   _____

   _____

   _____

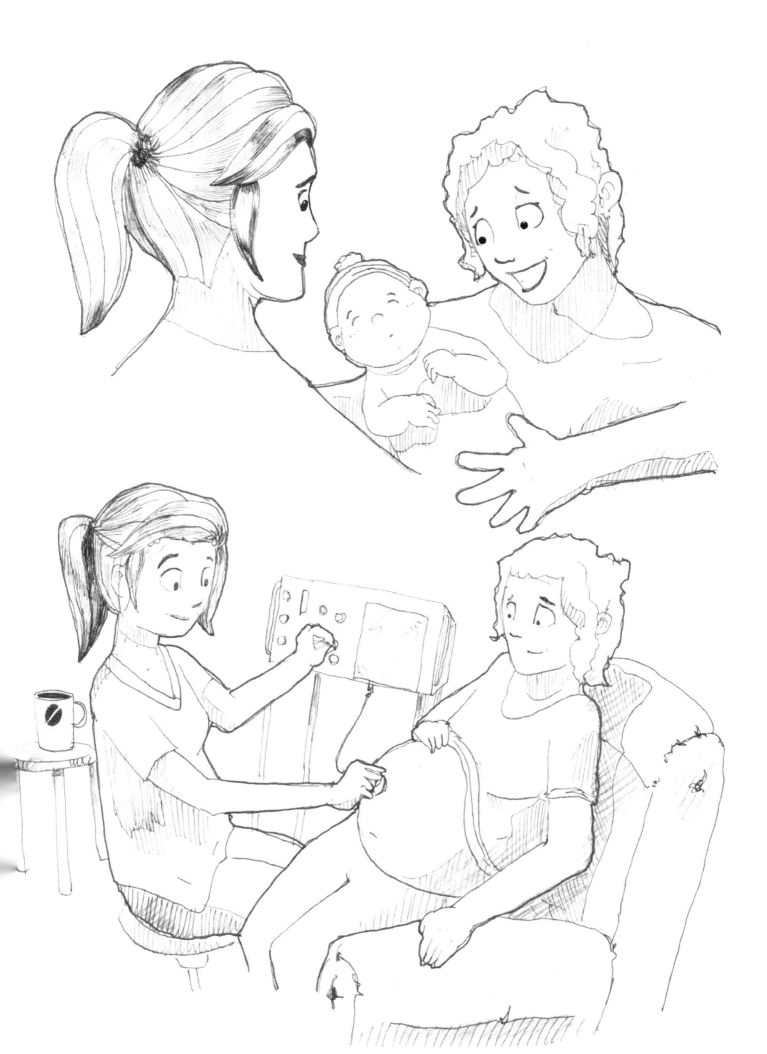

# THINKING QUESTIONS

1. What is this profession called?

   _____

   _____

2. What would the world be like if no one did this job?

   _____

   _____

   _____

3. What is a person with this job expected to accomplish?

   _____

   _____

   _____

4. Could you be good at this job? _____ Why?

   _____

   _____

   _____

5. What kind of education, ability, training and experience does a person need to do this job well?

   _____

   _____

   _____

6. How much money can a person earn when they do this job as a profession?

   _____

7. How much time does this job require?

   _____

8. Do you know someone with this job?

   _____

9. On a scale from one to ten, rate this job. 1 2 3 4 5 6 7 8 9 10

10. What is the best thing about this job and the worst thing about this job?

    _____

    _____

    _____

    _____

    _____

    _____

# THINKING QUESTIONS

1. What is this profession called?

   ----------------------------------------
   ----------------------------------------

2. What would the world be like if no one did this job?

   ----------------------------------------
   ----------------------------------------
   ----------------------------------------

3. What is a person with this job expected to accomplish?

   ----------------------------------------
   ----------------------------------------
   ----------------------------------------

4. Could you be good at this job? _____ Why?

   ----------------------------------------
   ----------------------------------------
   ----------------------------------------

5. What kind of education, ability, training and experience does a person need to do this job well?

   ----------------------------------------
   ----------------------------------------
   ----------------------------------------

6. How much money can a person earn when they do this job as a profession?

   ----------------------------------------

7. How much time does this job require?

   ----------------------------------------

8. Do you know someone with this job?

   ----------------------------------------

9. On a scale from one to ten, rate this job. 1 2 3 4 5 6 7 8 9 10

10. What is the best thing about this job and the worst thing about this job?

   ----------------------------------------
   ----------------------------------------
   ----------------------------------------
   ----------------------------------------
   ----------------------------------------
   ----------------------------------------

# THINKING QUESTIONS

1. What is this profession called?

   -------------------------------------------------------------------
   -------------------------------------------------------------------

2. What would the world be like if no one did this job?

   -------------------------------------------------------------------
   -------------------------------------------------------------------
   -------------------------------------------------------------------

3. What is a person with this job expected to accomplish?

   -------------------------------------------------------------------
   -------------------------------------------------------------------
   -------------------------------------------------------------------

4. Could you be good at this job? _____ Why?

   -------------------------------------------------------------------
   -------------------------------------------------------------------
   -------------------------------------------------------------------

5. What kind of education, ability, training and experience does a person need to do this job well?

   -------------------------------------------------------------------
   -------------------------------------------------------------------
   -------------------------------------------------------------------

6. How much money can a person earn when they do this job as a profession?

   -------------------------------------------------------------------

7. How much time does this job require?

   -------------------------------------------------------------------

8. Do you know someone with this job?

   -------------------------------------------------------------------

9. On a scale from one to ten, rate this job. 1 2 3 4 5 6 7 8 9 10
10. What is the best thing about this job and the worst thing about this job?

    -------------------------------------------------------------------
    -------------------------------------------------------------------
    -------------------------------------------------------------------
    -------------------------------------------------------------------
    -------------------------------------------------------------------
    -------------------------------------------------------------------

# THINKING QUESTIONS

1. What is this profession called?

   ------------------------------------------------------------

   ------------------------------------------------------------

2. What would the world be like if no one did this job?

   ------------------------------------------------------------

   ------------------------------------------------------------

   ------------------------------------------------------------

3. What is a person with this job expected to accomplish?

   ------------------------------------------------------------

   ------------------------------------------------------------

   ------------------------------------------------------------

4. Could you be good at this job? _____ Why?

   ------------------------------------------------------------

   ------------------------------------------------------------

   ------------------------------------------------------------

5. What  kind of education, ability, training and experience does a person need to do this job well?

   ------------------------------------------------------------

   ------------------------------------------------------------

   ------------------------------------------------------------

6. How much money can a person earn when they do this job as a profession?

   ------------------------------------------------------------

7. How much time does this job require?

   ------------------------------------------------------------

8. Do you know someone with this job?

   ------------------------------------------------------------

9. On a scale from one to ten, rate this job. 1 2 3 4 5 6 7 8 9 10

10. What is the best thing about this job and the worst thing about this job?

    ------------------------------------------------------------

    ------------------------------------------------------------

    ------------------------------------------------------------

    ------------------------------------------------------------

    ------------------------------------------------------------

    ------------------------------------------------------------

# THINKING QUESTIONS

1.  What is this profession called?

    ------------------------------------------------

    ------------------------------------------------

2.  What would the world be like if no one did this job?

    ------------------------------------------------

    ------------------------------------------------

    ------------------------------------------------

3.  What is a person with this job expected to accomplish?

    ------------------------------------------------

    ------------------------------------------------

    ------------------------------------------------

4.  Could you be good at this job? _____ Why?

    ------------------------------------------------

    ------------------------------------------------

    ------------------------------------------------

5.  What kind of education, ability, training and experience does a person need to do this job well?

    ------------------------------------------------

    ------------------------------------------------

    ------------------------------------------------

6.  How much money can a person earn when they do this job as a profession?

    ------------------------------------------------

7.  How much time does this job require?

    ------------------------------------------------

8.  Do you know someone with this job?

    ------------------------------------------------

9.  On a scale from one to ten, rate this job. 1 2 3 4 5 6 7 8 9 10
10. What is the best thing about this job and the worst thing about this job?

    ------------------------------------------------

    ------------------------------------------------

    ------------------------------------------------

    ------------------------------------------------

    ------------------------------------------------

    ------------------------------------------------

# THINKING QUESTIONS

1. What is this profession called?

   ------------------------------------------------

   ------------------------------------------------

2. What would the world be like if no one did this job?

   ------------------------------------------------

   ------------------------------------------------

   ------------------------------------------------

3. What is a person with this job expected to accomplish?

   ------------------------------------------------

   ------------------------------------------------

   ------------------------------------------------

4. Could you be good at this job? _____ Why?

   ------------------------------------------------

   ------------------------------------------------

   ------------------------------------------------

5. What kind of education, ability, training and experience does a person need to do this job well?

   ------------------------------------------------

   ------------------------------------------------

   ------------------------------------------------

6. How much money can a person earn when they do this job as a profession?

   ------------------------------------------------

7. How much time does this job require?

   ------------------------------------------------

8. Do you know someone with this job?

   ------------------------------------------------

9. On a scale from one to ten, rate this job. 1 2 3 4 5 6 7 8 9 10

10. What is the best thing about this job and the worst thing about this job?

    ------------------------------------------------

    ------------------------------------------------

    ------------------------------------------------

    ------------------------------------------------

    ------------------------------------------------

    ------------------------------------------------

# THINKING QUESTIONS

1. What is this profession called?

   ----------------------------------------------------------------
   ----------------------------------------------------------------

2. What would the world be like if no one did this job?

   ----------------------------------------------------------------
   ----------------------------------------------------------------
   ----------------------------------------------------------------

3. What is a person with this job expected to accomplish?

   ----------------------------------------------------------------
   ----------------------------------------------------------------
   ----------------------------------------------------------------

4. Could you be good at this job? _____ Why?

   ----------------------------------------------------------------
   ----------------------------------------------------------------
   ----------------------------------------------------------------

5. What kind of education, ability, training and experience does a person need to do this job well?

   ----------------------------------------------------------------
   ----------------------------------------------------------------
   ----------------------------------------------------------------

6. How much money can a person earn when they do this job as a profession?

   ----------------------------------------------------------------

7. How much time does this job require?

   ----------------------------------------------------------------

8. Do you know someone with this job?

   ----------------------------------------------------------------

9. On a scale from one to ten, rate this job. 1 2 3 4 5 6 7 8 9 10

10. What is the best thing about this job and the worst thing about this job?

    ----------------------------------------------------------------
    ----------------------------------------------------------------
    ----------------------------------------------------------------
    ----------------------------------------------------------------
    ----------------------------------------------------------------
    ----------------------------------------------------------------

# THINKING QUESTIONS

1.  What is this profession called?

    ------------------------------------------------

    ------------------------------------------------

2.  What would the world be like if no one did this job?

    ------------------------------------------------

    ------------------------------------------------

    ------------------------------------------------

3.  What is a person with this job expected to accomplish?

    ------------------------------------------------

    ------------------------------------------------

    ------------------------------------------------

4.  Could you be good at this job? _____ Why?

    ------------------------------------------------

    ------------------------------------------------

    ------------------------------------------------

5.  What kind of education, ability, training and experience does a person need to do this job well?

    ------------------------------------------------

    ------------------------------------------------

    ------------------------------------------------

6.  How much money can a person earn when they do this job as a profession?

    ------------------------------------------------

7.  How much time does this job require?

    ------------------------------------------------

8.  Do you know someone with this job?

    ------------------------------------------------

9.  On a scale from one to ten, rate this job. 1 2 3 4 5 6 7 8 9 10
10. What is the best thing about this job and the worst thing about this job?

    ------------------------------------------------

    ------------------------------------------------

    ------------------------------------------------

    ------------------------------------------------

    ------------------------------------------------

    ------------------------------------------------

# THINKING QUESTIONS

1. What is this profession called?

   -------------------------------------------------------------

   -------------------------------------------------------------

2. What would the world be like if no one did this job?

   -------------------------------------------------------------

   -------------------------------------------------------------

   -------------------------------------------------------------

3. What is a person with this job expected to accomplish?

   -------------------------------------------------------------

   -------------------------------------------------------------

   -------------------------------------------------------------

4. Could you be good at this job? _____ Why?

   -------------------------------------------------------------

   -------------------------------------------------------------

   -------------------------------------------------------------

5. What kind of education, ability, training and experience does a person need to do this job well?

   -------------------------------------------------------------

   -------------------------------------------------------------

   -------------------------------------------------------------

6. How much money can a person earn when they do this job as a profession?

   -------------------------------------------------------------

7. How much time does this job require?

   -------------------------------------------------------------

8. Do you know someone with this job?

   -------------------------------------------------------------

9. On a scale from one to ten, rate this job. 1 2 3 4 5 6 7 8 9 10
10. What is the best thing about this job and the worst thing about this job?

    -------------------------------------------------------------

    -------------------------------------------------------------

    -------------------------------------------------------------

    -------------------------------------------------------------

    -------------------------------------------------------------

    -------------------------------------------------------------

# THINKING QUESTIONS

1. What is this profession called?

   ----------------------------------------------------------------

2. What would the world be like if no one did this job?

   ----------------------------------------------------------------

   ----------------------------------------------------------------

3. What is a person with this job expected to accomplish?

   ----------------------------------------------------------------

   ----------------------------------------------------------------

4. Could you be good at this job? _____ Why?

   ----------------------------------------------------------------

   ----------------------------------------------------------------

5. What kind of education, ability, training and experience does a person need to do this job well?

   ----------------------------------------------------------------

   ----------------------------------------------------------------

6. How much money can a person earn when they do this job as a profession?

   ----------------------------------------------------------------

7. How much time does this job require?

   ----------------------------------------------------------------

8. Do you know someone with this job?

   ----------------------------------------------------------------

9. On a scale from one to ten, rate this job. 1 2 3 4 5 6 7 8 9 10

10. What is the best thing about this job and the worst thing about this job?

    ----------------------------------------------------------------

    ----------------------------------------------------------------

    ----------------------------------------------------------------

    ----------------------------------------------------------------

    ----------------------------------------------------------------

# THINKING QUESTIONS

1. What is this profession called?

   ------------------------------------------------

   ------------------------------------------------

2. What would the world be like if no one did this job?

   ------------------------------------------------

   ------------------------------------------------

   ------------------------------------------------

3. What is a person with this job expected to accomplish?

   ------------------------------------------------

   ------------------------------------------------

   ------------------------------------------------

4. Could you be good at this job? _____ Why?

   ------------------------------------------------

   ------------------------------------------------

   ------------------------------------------------

5. What kind of education, ability, training and experience does a person need to do this job well?

   ------------------------------------------------

   ------------------------------------------------

   ------------------------------------------------

6. How much money can a person earn when they do this job as a profession?

   ------------------------------------------------

7. How much time does this job require?

   ------------------------------------------------

8. Do you know someone with this job?

   ------------------------------------------------

9. On a scale from one to ten, rate this job. 1 2 3 4 5 6 7 8 9 10
10. What is the best thing about this job and the worst thing about this job?

   ------------------------------------------------

   ------------------------------------------------

   ------------------------------------------------

   ------------------------------------------------

   ------------------------------------------------

# THINKING QUESTIONS

1. What is this profession called?

   _____

   _____

2. What would the world be like if no one did this job?

   _____

   _____

   _____

3. What is a person with this job expected to accomplish?

   _____

   _____

   _____

4. Could you be good at this job? _____ Why?

   _____

   _____

   _____

5. What kind of education, ability, training and experience does a person need to do this job well?

   _____

   _____

   _____

6. How much money can a person earn when they do this job as a profession?

   _____

7. How much time does this job require?

   _____

8. Do you know someone with this job?

   _____

9. On a scale from one to ten, rate this job. 1 2 3 4 5 6 7 8 9 10

10. What is the best thing about this job and the worst thing about this job?

   _____

   _____

   _____

   _____

   _____

   _____

# THINKING QUESTIONS

1. What is this profession called?

   _____

   _____

2. What would the world be like if no one did this job?

   _____

   _____

   _____

3. What is a person with this job expected to accomplish?

   _____

   _____

   _____

4. Could you be good at this job? _____ Why?

   _____

   _____

   _____

5. What kind of education, ability, training and experience does a person need to do this job well?

   _____

   _____

   _____

6. How much money can a person earn when they do this job as a profession?

   _____

7. How much time does this job require?

   _____

8. Do you know someone with this job?

   _____

9. On a scale from one to ten, rate this job. 1 2 3 4 5 6 7 8 9 10

10. What is the best thing about this job and the worst thing about this job?

    _____

    _____

    _____

    _____

    _____

# THINKING QUESTIONS

1.  What is this profession called?

    _____

    _____

2.  What would the world be like if no one did this job?

    _____

    _____

    _____

3.  What is a person with this job expected to accomplish?

    _____

    _____

    _____

4.  Could you be good at this job? _____ Why?

    _____

    _____

    _____

5.  What kind of education, ability, training and experience does a person need to do this job well?

    _____

    _____

    _____

6.  How much money can a person earn when they do this job as a profession?

    _____

7.  How much time does this job require?

    _____

8.  Do you know someone with this job?

    _____

9.  On a scale from one to ten, rate this job. 1 2 3 4 5 6 7 8 9 10

10. What is the best thing about this job and the worst thing about this job?

    _____

    _____

    _____

    _____

    _____

    _____

# THINKING QUESTIONS

1. What is this profession called?

   _____

   _____

2. What would the world be like if no one did this job?

   _____

   _____

   _____

3. What is a person with this job expected to accomplish?

   _____

   _____

   _____

4. Could you be good at this job? _____ Why?

   _____

   _____

   _____

5. What kind of education, ability, training and experience does a person need to do this job well?

   _____

   _____

   _____

6. How much money can a person earn when they do this job as a profession?

   _____

7. How much time does this job require?

   _____

8. Do you know someone with this job?

   _____

9. On a scale from one to ten, rate this job. 1 2 3 4 5 6 7 8 9 10

10. What is the best thing about this job and the worst thing about this job?

    _____

    _____

    _____

    _____

    _____

    _____

# THINKING QUESTIONS

1. What is this profession called?

   ------------------------------------------------
   ------------------------------------------------

2. What would the world be like if no one did this job?

   ------------------------------------------------
   ------------------------------------------------
   ------------------------------------------------

3. What is a person with this job expected to accomplish?

   ------------------------------------------------
   ------------------------------------------------
   ------------------------------------------------

4. Could you be good at this job? _____ Why?

   ------------------------------------------------
   ------------------------------------------------
   ------------------------------------------------

5. What kind of education, ability, training and experience does a person need to do this job well?

   ------------------------------------------------
   ------------------------------------------------
   ------------------------------------------------

6. How much money can a person earn when they do this job as a profession?

   ------------------------------------------------

7. How much time does this job require?

   ------------------------------------------------

8. Do you know someone with this job?

   ------------------------------------------------

9. On a scale from one to ten, rate this job. 1 2 3 4 5 6 7 8 9 10

10. What is the best thing about this job and the worst thing about this job?

   ------------------------------------------------
   ------------------------------------------------
   ------------------------------------------------
   ------------------------------------------------
   ------------------------------------------------
   ------------------------------------------------

# THINKING QUESTIONS

1.  What is this profession called?

    ---------------------------------------------------------------
    ---------------------------------------------------------------

2.  What would the world be like if no one did this job?

    ---------------------------------------------------------------
    ---------------------------------------------------------------
    ---------------------------------------------------------------

3.  What is a person with this job expected to accomplish?

    ---------------------------------------------------------------
    ---------------------------------------------------------------
    ---------------------------------------------------------------

4.  Could you be good at this job? _____ Why?

    ---------------------------------------------------------------
    ---------------------------------------------------------------
    ---------------------------------------------------------------

5.  What kind of education, ability, training and experience does a person need to do this job well?

    ---------------------------------------------------------------
    ---------------------------------------------------------------
    ---------------------------------------------------------------

6.  How much money can a person earn when they do this job as a profession?

    ---------------------------------------------------------------

7.  How much time does this job require?

    ---------------------------------------------------------------

8.  Do you know someone with this job?

    ---------------------------------------------------------------

9.  On a scale from one to ten, rate this job. 1 2 3 4 5 6 7 8 9 10
10. What is the best thing about this job and the worst thing about this job?

    ---------------------------------------------------------------
    ---------------------------------------------------------------
    ---------------------------------------------------------------
    ---------------------------------------------------------------
    ---------------------------------------------------------------
    ---------------------------------------------------------------

# THINKING QUESTIONS

1. What is this profession called?

   ------------------------------------------------

   ------------------------------------------------

2. What would the world be like if no one did this job?

   ------------------------------------------------

   ------------------------------------------------

   ------------------------------------------------

3. What is a person with this job expected to accomplish?

   ------------------------------------------------

   ------------------------------------------------

   ------------------------------------------------

4. Could you be good at this job? _____ Why?

   ------------------------------------------------

   ------------------------------------------------

   ------------------------------------------------

5. What kind of education, ability, training and experience does a person need to do this job well?

   ------------------------------------------------

   ------------------------------------------------

   ------------------------------------------------

6. How much money can a person earn when they do this job as a profession?

   ------------------------------------------------

7. How much time does this job require?

   ------------------------------------------------

8. Do you know someone with this job?

   ------------------------------------------------

9. On a scale from one to ten, rate this job. 1 2 3 4 5 6 7 8 9 10

10. What is the best thing about this job and the worst thing about this job?

   ------------------------------------------------

   ------------------------------------------------

   ------------------------------------------------

   ------------------------------------------------

   ------------------------------------------------

   ------------------------------------------------

# THINKING QUESTIONS

1. What is this profession called?

   ------------------------------------------------
   ------------------------------------------------

2. What would the world be like if no one did this job?

   ------------------------------------------------
   ------------------------------------------------
   ------------------------------------------------

3. What is a person with this job expected to accomplish?

   ------------------------------------------------
   ------------------------------------------------
   ------------------------------------------------

4. Could you be good at this job? _____ Why?

   ------------------------------------------------
   ------------------------------------------------
   ------------------------------------------------

5. What kind of education, ability, training and experience does a person need to do this job well?

   ------------------------------------------------
   ------------------------------------------------
   ------------------------------------------------

6. How much money can a person earn when they do this job as a profession?

   ------------------------------------------------

7. How much time does this job require?

   ------------------------------------------------

8. Do you know someone with this job?

   ------------------------------------------------

9. On a scale from one to ten, rate this job. 1 2 3 4 5 6 7 8 9 10
10. What is the best thing about this job and the worst thing about this job?

   ------------------------------------------------
   ------------------------------------------------
   ------------------------------------------------
   ------------------------------------------------
   ------------------------------------------------
   ------------------------------------------------

# THINKING QUESTIONS

1. What is this profession called?

   ----------------------------------------------------------------

   ----------------------------------------------------------------

2. What would the world be like if no one did this job?

   ----------------------------------------------------------------

   ----------------------------------------------------------------

   ----------------------------------------------------------------

3. What is a person with this job expected to accomplish?

   ----------------------------------------------------------------

   ----------------------------------------------------------------

   ----------------------------------------------------------------

4. Could you be good at this job? _____ Why?

   ----------------------------------------------------------------

   ----------------------------------------------------------------

   ----------------------------------------------------------------

5. What kind of education, ability, training and experience does a person need to do this job well?

   ----------------------------------------------------------------

   ----------------------------------------------------------------

   ----------------------------------------------------------------

6. How much money can a person earn when they do this job as a profession?

   ----------------------------------------------------------------

7. How much time does this job require?

   ----------------------------------------------------------------

8. Do you know someone with this job?

   ----------------------------------------------------------------

9. On a scale from one to ten, rate this job. 1 2 3 4 5 6 7 8 9 10

10. What is the best thing about this job and the worst thing about this job?

   ----------------------------------------------------------------

   ----------------------------------------------------------------

   ----------------------------------------------------------------

   ----------------------------------------------------------------

   ----------------------------------------------------------------

   ----------------------------------------------------------------

# THINKING QUESTIONS

1. What is this profession called?

   ------------------------------------------------

   ------------------------------------------------

2. What would the world be like if no one did this job?

   ------------------------------------------------

   ------------------------------------------------

   ------------------------------------------------

3. What is a person with this job expected to accomplish?

   ------------------------------------------------

   ------------------------------------------------

   ------------------------------------------------

4. Could you be good at this job? _____ Why?

   ------------------------------------------------

   ------------------------------------------------

   ------------------------------------------------

5. What kind of education, ability, training and experience does a person need to do this job well?

   ------------------------------------------------

   ------------------------------------------------

   ------------------------------------------------

6. How much money can a person earn when they do this job as a profession?

   ------------------------------------------------

7. How much time does this job require?

   ------------------------------------------------

8. Do you know someone with this job?

   ------------------------------------------------

9. On a scale from one to ten, rate this job. 1 2 3 4 5 6 7 8 9 10

10. What is the best thing about this job and the worst thing about this job?

    ------------------------------------------------

    ------------------------------------------------

    ------------------------------------------------

    ------------------------------------------------

    ------------------------------------------------

    ------------------------------------------------

# THINKING QUESTIONS

1. What is this profession called?

   _____

   _____

2. What would the world be like if no one did this job?

   _____

   _____

   _____

3. What is a person with this job expected to accomplish?

   _____

   _____

   _____

4. Could you be good at this job? _____ Why?

   _____

   _____

   _____

5. What  kind of education, ability, training and experience does a person need to do this job well?

   _____

   _____

   _____

6. How much money can a person earn when they do this job as a profession?

   _____

7. How much time does this job require?

   _____

8. Do you know someone with this job?

   _____

9. On a scale from one to ten, rate this job. 1 2 3 4 5 6 7 8 9 10

10. What is the best thing about this job and the worst thing about this job?

   _____

   _____

   _____

   _____

   _____

   _____

# THINKING QUESTIONS

1. What is this profession called?

   ------------------------------------------------------------

   ------------------------------------------------------------

2. What would the world be like if no one did this job?

   ------------------------------------------------------------

   ------------------------------------------------------------

   ------------------------------------------------------------

3. What is a person with this job expected to accomplish?

   ------------------------------------------------------------

   ------------------------------------------------------------

   ------------------------------------------------------------

4. Could you be good at this job? _____ Why?

   ------------------------------------------------------------

   ------------------------------------------------------------

   ------------------------------------------------------------

5. What kind of education, ability, training and experience does a person need to do this job well?

   ------------------------------------------------------------

   ------------------------------------------------------------

   ------------------------------------------------------------

6. How much money can a person earn when they do this job as a profession?

   ------------------------------------------------------------

7. How much time does this job require?

   ------------------------------------------------------------

8. Do you know someone with this job?

   ------------------------------------------------------------

9. On a scale from one to ten, rate this job. 1 2 3 4 5 6 7 8 9 10
10. What is the best thing about this job and the worst thing about this job?

   ------------------------------------------------------------

   ------------------------------------------------------------

   ------------------------------------------------------------

   ------------------------------------------------------------

   ------------------------------------------------------------

# THINKING QUESTIONS

1. What is this profession called?

   ------------------------------------------------

   ------------------------------------------------

2. What would the world be like if no one did this job?

   ------------------------------------------------

   ------------------------------------------------

   ------------------------------------------------

3. What is a person with this job expected to accomplish?

   ------------------------------------------------

   ------------------------------------------------

   ------------------------------------------------

4. Could you be good at this job? _____ Why?

   ------------------------------------------------

   ------------------------------------------------

   ------------------------------------------------

5. What kind of education, ability, training and experience does a person need to do this job well?

   ------------------------------------------------

   ------------------------------------------------

   ------------------------------------------------

6. How much money can a person earn when they do this job as a profession?

   ------------------------------------------------

7. How much time does this job require?

   ------------------------------------------------

8. Do you know someone with this job?

   ------------------------------------------------

9. On a scale from one to ten, rate this job. 1 2 3 4 5 6 7 8 9 10

10. What is the best thing about this job and the worst thing about this job?

    ------------------------------------------------

    ------------------------------------------------

    ------------------------------------------------

    ------------------------------------------------

    ------------------------------------------------

# THINKING QUESTIONS

1.  What is this profession called?

    ------------------------------------------------
    ------------------------------------------------

2.  What would the world be like if no one did this job?

    ------------------------------------------------
    ------------------------------------------------
    ------------------------------------------------

3.  What is a person with this job expected to accomplish?

    ------------------------------------------------
    ------------------------------------------------
    ------------------------------------------------

4.  Could you be good at this job? _____ Why?

    ------------------------------------------------
    ------------------------------------------------
    ------------------------------------------------

5.  What kind of education, ability, training and experience does a person need to do this job well?

    ------------------------------------------------
    ------------------------------------------------
    ------------------------------------------------

6.  How much money can a person earn when they do this job as a profession?

    ------------------------------------------------

7.  How much time does this job require?

    ------------------------------------------------

8.  Do you know someone with this job?

    ------------------------------------------------

9.  On a scale from one to ten, rate this job. 1 2 3 4 5 6 7 8 9 10

10. What is the best thing about this job and the worst thing about this job?

    ------------------------------------------------
    ------------------------------------------------
    ------------------------------------------------
    ------------------------------------------------
    ------------------------------------------------
    ------------------------------------------------

# THINKING QUESTIONS

1.  What is this profession called?

    _____

    _____

2.  What would the world be like if no one did this job?

    _____

    _____

    _____

3.  What is a person with this job expected to accomplish?

    _____

    _____

    _____

4.  Could you be good at this job? _____ Why?

    _____

    _____

    _____

5.  What kind of education, ability, training and experience does a person need to do this job well?

    _____

    _____

    _____

6.  How much money can a person earn when they do this job as a profession?

    _____

7.  How much time does this job require?

    _____

8.  Do you know someone with this job?

    _____

9.  On a scale from one to ten, rate this job. 1 2 3 4 5 6 7 8 9 10

10. What is the best thing about this job and the worst thing about this job?

    _____

    _____

    _____

    _____

    _____

    _____

# THINKING QUESTIONS

1. What is this profession called?

   _____

   _____

2. What would the world be like if no one did this job?

   _____

   _____

   _____

3. What is a person with this job expected to accomplish?

   _____

   _____

   _____

4. Could you be good at this job? _____ Why?

   _____

   _____

   _____

5. What kind of education, ability, training and experience does a person need to do this job well?

   _____

   _____

   _____

6. How much money can a person earn when they do this job as a profession?

   _____

7. How much time does this job require?

   _____

8. Do you know someone with this job?

   _____

9. On a scale from one to ten, rate this job. 1 2 3 4 5 6 7 8 9 10

10. What is the best thing about this job and the worst thing about this job?

    _____

    _____

    _____

    _____

    _____

    _____

# THINKING QUESTIONS

1. What is this profession called?

   ------------------------------------------------

   ------------------------------------------------

2. What would the world be like if no one did this job?

   ------------------------------------------------

   ------------------------------------------------

   ------------------------------------------------

3. What is a person with this job expected to accomplish?

   ------------------------------------------------

   ------------------------------------------------

   ------------------------------------------------

4. Could you be good at this job? _____ Why?

   ------------------------------------------------

   ------------------------------------------------

   ------------------------------------------------

5. What kind of education, ability, training and experience does a person need to do this job well?

   ------------------------------------------------

   ------------------------------------------------

   ------------------------------------------------

6. How much money can a person earn when they do this job as a profession?

   ------------------------------------------------

7. How much time does this job require?

   ------------------------------------------------

8. Do you know someone with this job?

   ------------------------------------------------

9. On a scale from one to ten, rate this job. 1 2 3 4 5 6 7 8 9 10
10. What is the best thing about this job and the worst thing about this job?

    ------------------------------------------------

    ------------------------------------------------

    ------------------------------------------------

    ------------------------------------------------

    ------------------------------------------------

# THINKING QUESTIONS

1. What is this profession called?

   ---------------------------------------------------------------
   ---------------------------------------------------------------

2. What would the world be like if no one did this job?

   ---------------------------------------------------------------
   ---------------------------------------------------------------
   ---------------------------------------------------------------

3. What is a person with this job expected to accomplish?

   ---------------------------------------------------------------
   ---------------------------------------------------------------
   ---------------------------------------------------------------

4. Could you be good at this job? _____ Why?

   ---------------------------------------------------------------
   ---------------------------------------------------------------
   ---------------------------------------------------------------

5. What kind of education, ability, training and experience does a person need to do this job well?

   ---------------------------------------------------------------
   ---------------------------------------------------------------
   ---------------------------------------------------------------

6. How much money can a person earn when they do this job as a profession?

   ---------------------------------------------------------------

7. How much time does this job require?

   ---------------------------------------------------------------

8. Do you know someone with this job?

   ---------------------------------------------------------------

9. On a scale from one to ten, rate this job. 1 2 3 4 5 6 7 8 9 10

10. What is the best thing about this job and the worst thing about this job?

    ---------------------------------------------------------------
    ---------------------------------------------------------------
    ---------------------------------------------------------------
    ---------------------------------------------------------------
    ---------------------------------------------------------------
    ---------------------------------------------------------------

# THINKING QUESTIONS

1.  What is this profession called?

    ------------------------------------------------

    ------------------------------------------------

2.  What would the world be like if no one did this job?

    ------------------------------------------------

    ------------------------------------------------

    ------------------------------------------------

3.  What is a person with this job expected to accomplish?

    ------------------------------------------------

    ------------------------------------------------

    ------------------------------------------------

4.  Could you be good at this job? _____ Why?

    ------------------------------------------------

    ------------------------------------------------

    ------------------------------------------------

5.  What kind of education, ability, training and experience does a person need to do this job well?

    ------------------------------------------------

    ------------------------------------------------

    ------------------------------------------------

6.  How much money can a person earn when they do this job as a profession?

    ------------------------------------------------

7.  How much time does this job require?

    ------------------------------------------------

8.  Do you know someone with this job?

    ------------------------------------------------

9.  On a scale from one to ten, rate this job. 1 2 3 4 5 6 7 8 9 10
10. What is the best thing about this job and the worst thing about this job?

    ------------------------------------------------

    ------------------------------------------------

    ------------------------------------------------

    ------------------------------------------------

    ------------------------------------------------

    ------------------------------------------------

# THINKING QUESTIONS

1. What is this profession called?

   _____

   _____

2. What would the world be like if no one did this job?

   _____

   _____

   _____

3. What is a person with this job expected to accomplish?

   _____

   _____

   _____

4. Could you be good at this job? _____ Why?

   _____

   _____

   _____

5. What kind of education, ability, training and experience does a person need to do this job well?

   _____

   _____

   _____

6. How much money can a person earn when they do this job as a profession?

   _____

7. How much time does this job require?

   _____

8. Do you know someone with this job?

   _____

9. On a scale from one to ten, rate this job. 1 2 3 4 5 6 7 8 9 10

10. What is the best thing about this job and the worst thing about this job?

   _____

   _____

   _____

   _____

   _____

# THINKING QUESTIONS

1. What is this profession called?

   ----------------------------------------

   ----------------------------------------

2. What would the world be like if no one did this job?

   ----------------------------------------

   ----------------------------------------

   ----------------------------------------

3. What is a person with this job expected to accomplish?

   ----------------------------------------

   ----------------------------------------

   ----------------------------------------

4. Could you be good at this job? _____ Why?

   ----------------------------------------

   ----------------------------------------

   ----------------------------------------

5. What kind of education, ability, training and experience does a person need to do this job well?

   ----------------------------------------

   ----------------------------------------

   ----------------------------------------

6. How much money can a person earn when they do this job as a profession?

   ----------------------------------------

7. How much time does this job require?

   ----------------------------------------

8. Do you know someone with this job?

   ----------------------------------------

9. On a scale from one to ten, rate this job. 1 2 3 4 5 6 7 8 9 10

10. What is the best thing about this job and the worst thing about this job?

   ----------------------------------------

   ----------------------------------------

   ----------------------------------------

   ----------------------------------------

   ----------------------------------------

   ----------------------------------------

# THINKING QUESTIONS

1. What is this profession called?

   _____

   _____

2. What would the world be like if no one did this job?

   _____

   _____

   _____

3. What is a person with this job expected to accomplish?

   _____

   _____

   _____

4. Could you be good at this job? _____ Why?

   _____

   _____

   _____

5. What kind of education, ability, training and experience does a person need to do this job well?

   _____

   _____

   _____

6. How much money can a person earn when they do this job as a profession?

   _____

7. How much time does this job require?

   _____

8. Do you know someone with this job?

   _____

9. On a scale from one to ten, rate this job. 1 2 3 4 5 6 7 8 9 10

10. What is the best thing about this job and the worst thing about this job?

    _____

    _____

    _____

    _____

    _____

# THINKING QUESTIONS

1.  What is this profession called?

    ------------------------------------------------

    ------------------------------------------------

2.  What would the world be like if no one did this job?

    ------------------------------------------------

    ------------------------------------------------

    ------------------------------------------------

3.  What is a person with this job expected to accomplish?

    ------------------------------------------------

    ------------------------------------------------

    ------------------------------------------------

4.  Could you be good at this job? _____ Why?

    ------------------------------------------------

    ------------------------------------------------

    ------------------------------------------------

5.  What kind of education, ability, training and experience does a person need to do this job well?

    ------------------------------------------------

    ------------------------------------------------

    ------------------------------------------------

6.  How much money can a person earn when they do this job as a profession?

    ------------------------------------------------

7.  How much time does this job require?

    ------------------------------------------------

8.  Do you know someone with this job?

    ------------------------------------------------

9.  On a scale from one to ten, rate this job. 1 2 3 4 5 6 7 8 9 10

10. What is the best thing about this job and the worst thing about this job?

    ------------------------------------------------

    ------------------------------------------------

    ------------------------------------------------

    ------------------------------------------------

    ------------------------------------------------

    ------------------------------------------------

# THINKING QUESTIONS

1. What is this profession called?

   ------------------------------------------------

   ------------------------------------------------

2. What would the world be like if no one did this job?

   ------------------------------------------------

   ------------------------------------------------

   ------------------------------------------------

3. What is a person with this job expected to accomplish?

   ------------------------------------------------

   ------------------------------------------------

   ------------------------------------------------

4. Could you be good at this job? _____ Why?

   ------------------------------------------------

   ------------------------------------------------

   ------------------------------------------------

5. What kind of education, ability, training and experience does a person need to do this job well?

   ------------------------------------------------

   ------------------------------------------------

   ------------------------------------------------

6. How much money can a person earn when they do this job as a profession?

   ------------------------------------------------

7. How much time does this job require?

   ------------------------------------------------

8. Do you know someone with this job?

   ------------------------------------------------

9. On a scale from one to ten, rate this job. 1 2 3 4 5 6 7 8 9 10

10. What is the best thing about this job and the worst thing about this job?

    ------------------------------------------------

    ------------------------------------------------

    ------------------------------------------------

    ------------------------------------------------

    ------------------------------------------------

    ------------------------------------------------

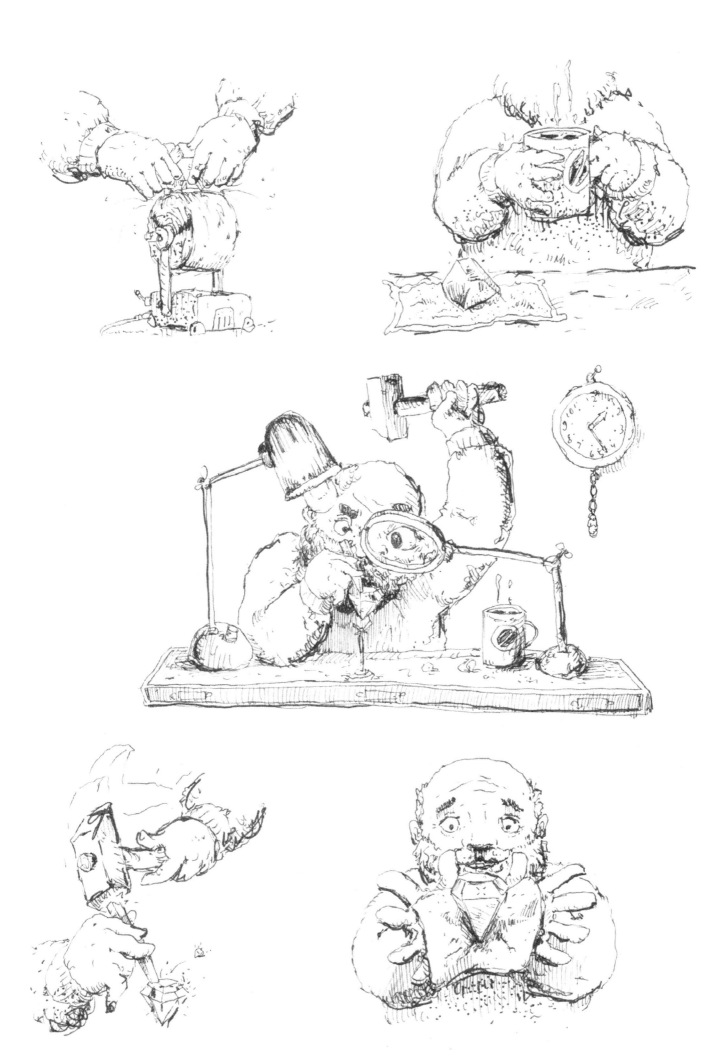

# THINKING QUESTIONS

1. What is this profession called?

   ----------------------------------------------

   ----------------------------------------------

2. What would the world be like if no one did this job?

   ----------------------------------------------

   ----------------------------------------------

   ----------------------------------------------

3. What is a person with this job expected to accomplish?

   ----------------------------------------------

   ----------------------------------------------

   ----------------------------------------------

4. Could you be good at this job? _____ Why?

   ----------------------------------------------

   ----------------------------------------------

   ----------------------------------------------

5. What kind of education, ability, training and experience does a person need to do this job well?

   ----------------------------------------------

   ----------------------------------------------

   ----------------------------------------------

6. How much money can a person earn when they do this job as a profession?

   ----------------------------------------------

7. How much time does this job require?

   ----------------------------------------------

8. Do you know someone with this job?

   ----------------------------------------------

9. On a scale from one to ten, rate this job. 1 2 3 4 5 6 7 8 9 10

10. What is the best thing about this job and the worst thing about this job?

   ----------------------------------------------

   ----------------------------------------------

   ----------------------------------------------

   ----------------------------------------------

   ----------------------------------------------

   ----------------------------------------------

# THINKING QUESTIONS

1. What is this profession called?

   _____

   _____

2. What would the world be like if no one did this job?

   _____

   _____

   _____

3. What is a person with this job expected to accomplish?

   _____

   _____

   _____

4. Could you be good at this job? _____ Why?

   _____

   _____

   _____

5. What kind of education, ability, training and experience does a person need to do this job well?

   _____

   _____

   _____

6. How much money can a person earn when they do this job as a profession?

   _____

7. How much time does this job require?

   _____

8. Do you know someone with this job?

   _____

9. On a scale from one to ten, rate this job. 1 2 3 4 5 6 7 8 9 10
10. What is the best thing about this job and the worst thing about this job?

   _____

   _____

   _____

   _____

   _____

   _____

# THINKING QUESTIONS

1.  What is this profession called?

    ----------------------------------------------

    ----------------------------------------------

2.  What would the world be like if no one did this job?

    ----------------------------------------------

    ----------------------------------------------

    ----------------------------------------------

3.  What is a person with this job expected to accomplish?

    ----------------------------------------------

    ----------------------------------------------

    ----------------------------------------------

4.  Could you be good at this job? _____ Why?

    ----------------------------------------------

    ----------------------------------------------

    ----------------------------------------------

5.  What kind of education, ability, training and experience does a person need to do this job well?

    ----------------------------------------------

    ----------------------------------------------

    ----------------------------------------------

6.  How much money can a person earn when they do this job as a profession?

    ----------------------------------------------

7.  How much time does this job require?

    ----------------------------------------------

8.  Do you know someone with this job?

    ----------------------------------------------

9.  On a scale from one to ten, rate this job. 1 2 3 4 5 6 7 8 9 10

10. What is the best thing about this job and the worst thing about this job?

    ----------------------------------------------

    ----------------------------------------------

    ----------------------------------------------

    ----------------------------------------------

    ----------------------------------------------

# THINKING QUESTIONS

1. What is this profession called?

   ------------------------------------------------------------

   ------------------------------------------------------------

2. What would the world be like if no one did this job?

   ------------------------------------------------------------

   ------------------------------------------------------------

   ------------------------------------------------------------

3. What is a person with this job expected to accomplish?

   ------------------------------------------------------------

   ------------------------------------------------------------

   ------------------------------------------------------------

4. Could you be good at this job? _____ Why?

   ------------------------------------------------------------

   ------------------------------------------------------------

   ------------------------------------------------------------

5. What kind of education, ability, training and experience does a person need to do this job well?

   ------------------------------------------------------------

   ------------------------------------------------------------

   ------------------------------------------------------------

6. How much money can a person earn when they do this job as a profession?

   ------------------------------------------------------------

7. How much time does this job require?

   ------------------------------------------------------------

8. Do you know someone with this job?

   ------------------------------------------------------------

9. On a scale from one to ten, rate this job. 1 2 3 4 5 6 7 8 9 10

10. What is the best thing about this job and the worst thing about this job?

    ------------------------------------------------------------

    ------------------------------------------------------------

    ------------------------------------------------------------

    ------------------------------------------------------------

    ------------------------------------------------------------

    ------------------------------------------------------------

# THINKING QUESTIONS

1. What is this profession called?

   --------------------------------------------------------

   --------------------------------------------------------

2. What would the world be like if no one did this job?

   --------------------------------------------------------

   --------------------------------------------------------

   --------------------------------------------------------

3. What is a person with this job expected to accomplish?

   --------------------------------------------------------

   --------------------------------------------------------

   --------------------------------------------------------

4. Could you be good at this job? _____ Why?

   --------------------------------------------------------

   --------------------------------------------------------

   --------------------------------------------------------

5. What kind of education, ability, training and experience does a person need to do this job well?

   --------------------------------------------------------

   --------------------------------------------------------

   --------------------------------------------------------

6. How much money can a person earn when they do this job as a profession?

   --------------------------------------------------------

7. How much time does this job require?

   --------------------------------------------------------

8. Do you know someone with this job?

   --------------------------------------------------------

9. On a scale from one to ten, rate this job. 1 2 3 4 5 6 7 8 9 10

10. What is the best thing about this job and the worst thing about this job?

   --------------------------------------------------------

   --------------------------------------------------------

   --------------------------------------------------------

   --------------------------------------------------------

   --------------------------------------------------------

   --------------------------------------------------------

# THINKING QUESTIONS

1. What is this profession called?

   ------------------------------------------------------------

   ------------------------------------------------------------

2. What would the world be like if no one did this job?

   ------------------------------------------------------------

   ------------------------------------------------------------

   ------------------------------------------------------------

3. What is a person with this job expected to accomplish?

   ------------------------------------------------------------

   ------------------------------------------------------------

   ------------------------------------------------------------

4. Could you be good at this job? _____ Why?

   ------------------------------------------------------------

   ------------------------------------------------------------

   ------------------------------------------------------------

5. What kind of education, ability, training and experience does a person need to do this job well?

   ------------------------------------------------------------

   ------------------------------------------------------------

   ------------------------------------------------------------

6. How much money can a person earn when they do this job as a profession?

   ------------------------------------------------------------

7. How much time does this job require?

   ------------------------------------------------------------

8. Do you know someone with this job?

   ------------------------------------------------------------

9. On a scale from one to ten, rate this job. 1 2 3 4 5 6 7 8 9 10

10. What is the best thing about this job and the worst thing about this job?

   ------------------------------------------------------------

   ------------------------------------------------------------

   ------------------------------------------------------------

   ------------------------------------------------------------

   ------------------------------------------------------------

   ------------------------------------------------------------

# THINKING QUESTIONS

1. What is this profession called?

   ------------------------------------------------

   ------------------------------------------------

2. What would the world be like if no one did this job?

   ------------------------------------------------

   ------------------------------------------------

   ------------------------------------------------

3. What is a person with this job expected to accomplish?

   ------------------------------------------------

   ------------------------------------------------

   ------------------------------------------------

4. Could you be good at this job? _____ Why?

   ------------------------------------------------

   ------------------------------------------------

   ------------------------------------------------

5. What kind of education, ability, training and experience does a person need to do this job well?

   ------------------------------------------------

   ------------------------------------------------

   ------------------------------------------------

6. How much money can a person earn when they do this job as a profession?

   ------------------------------------------------

7. How much time does this job require?

   ------------------------------------------------

8. Do you know someone with this job?

   ------------------------------------------------

9. On a scale from one to ten, rate this job. 1 2 3 4 5 6 7 8 9 10
10. What is the best thing about this job and the worst thing about this job?

    ------------------------------------------------

    ------------------------------------------------

    ------------------------------------------------

    ------------------------------------------------

    ------------------------------------------------

    ------------------------------------------------

# THINKING QUESTIONS

1. What is this profession called?

   ----------------------------------------------------------------

   ----------------------------------------------------------------

2. What would the world be like if no one did this job?

   ----------------------------------------------------------------

   ----------------------------------------------------------------

   ----------------------------------------------------------------

3. What is a person with this job expected to accomplish?

   ----------------------------------------------------------------

   ----------------------------------------------------------------

   ----------------------------------------------------------------

4. Could you be good at this job? _____ Why?

   ----------------------------------------------------------------

   ----------------------------------------------------------------

   ----------------------------------------------------------------

5. What kind of education, ability, training and experience does a person need to do this job well?

   ----------------------------------------------------------------

   ----------------------------------------------------------------

   ----------------------------------------------------------------

6. How much money can a person earn when they do this job as a profession?

   ----------------------------------------------------------------

7. How much time does this job require?

   ----------------------------------------------------------------

8. Do you know someone with this job?

   ----------------------------------------------------------------

9. On a scale from one to ten, rate this job. 1 2 3 4 5 6 7 8 9 10

10. What is the best thing about this job and the worst thing about this job?

   ----------------------------------------------------------------

   ----------------------------------------------------------------

   ----------------------------------------------------------------

   ----------------------------------------------------------------

   ----------------------------------------------------------------

# THINKING QUESTIONS

1.  What is this profession called?

    ------------------------------------------------------------

    ------------------------------------------------------------

2.  What would the world be like if no one did this job?

    ------------------------------------------------------------

    ------------------------------------------------------------

    ------------------------------------------------------------

3.  What is a person with this job expected to accomplish?

    ------------------------------------------------------------

    ------------------------------------------------------------

    ------------------------------------------------------------

4.  Could you be good at this job? _____ Why?

    ------------------------------------------------------------

    ------------------------------------------------------------

    ------------------------------------------------------------

5.  What kind of education, ability, training and experience does a person need to do this job well?

    ------------------------------------------------------------

    ------------------------------------------------------------

    ------------------------------------------------------------

6.  How much money can a person earn when they do this job as a profession?

    ------------------------------------------------------------

7.  How much time does this job require?

    ------------------------------------------------------------

8.  Do you know someone with this job?

    ------------------------------------------------------------

9.  On a scale from one to ten, rate this job. 1 2 3 4 5 6 7 8 9 10

10. What is the best thing about this job and the worst thing about this job?

    ------------------------------------------------------------

    ------------------------------------------------------------

    ------------------------------------------------------------

    ------------------------------------------------------------

    ------------------------------------------------------------

    ------------------------------------------------------------

# THINKING QUESTIONS

1. What is this profession called?

   _____

   _____

2. What would the world be like if no one did this job?

   _____

   _____

   _____

3. What is a person with this job expected to accomplish?

   _____

   _____

   _____

4. Could you be good at this job? _____ Why?

   _____

   _____

   _____

5. What kind of education, ability, training and experience does a person need to do this job well?

   _____

   _____

   _____

6. How much money can a person earn when they do this job as a profession?

   _____

7. How much time does this job require?

   _____

8. Do you know someone with this job?

   _____

9. On a scale from one to ten, rate this job. 1 2 3 4 5 6 7 8 9 10

10. What is the best thing about this job and the worst thing about this job?

    _____

    _____

    _____

    _____

    _____

# THINKING QUESTIONS

1. What is this profession called?

   _____

   _____

2. What would the world be like if no one did this job?

   _____

   _____

   _____

3. What is a person with this job expected to accomplish?

   _____

   _____

   _____

4. Could you be good at this job? _____ Why?

   _____

   _____

   _____

5. What kind of education, ability, training and experience does a person need to do this job well?

   _____

   _____

   _____

6. How much money can a person earn when they do this job as a profession?

   _____

7. How much time does this job require?

   _____

8. Do you know someone with this job?

   _____

9. On a scale from one to ten, rate this job. 1 2 3 4 5 6 7 8 9 10

10. What is the best thing about this job and the worst thing about this job?

    _____

    _____

    _____

    _____

    _____

    _____

# THINKING QUESTIONS

1. What is this profession called?

   ------------------------------------------------

   ------------------------------------------------

2. What would the world be like if no one did this job?

   ------------------------------------------------

   ------------------------------------------------

   ------------------------------------------------

3. What is a person with this job expected to accomplish?

   ------------------------------------------------

   ------------------------------------------------

   ------------------------------------------------

4. Could you be good at this job? _____ Why?

   ------------------------------------------------

   ------------------------------------------------

   ------------------------------------------------

5. What kind of education, ability, training and experience does a person need to do this job well?

   ------------------------------------------------

   ------------------------------------------------

   ------------------------------------------------

6. How much money can a person earn when they do this job as a profession?

   ------------------------------------------------

7. How much time does this job require?

   ------------------------------------------------

8. Do you know someone with this job?

   ------------------------------------------------

9. On a scale from one to ten, rate this job. 1 2 3 4 5 6 7 8 9 10

10. What is the best thing about this job and the worst thing about this job?

   ------------------------------------------------

   ------------------------------------------------

   ------------------------------------------------

   ------------------------------------------------

   ------------------------------------------------

   ------------------------------------------------

# THINKING QUESTIONS

1. What is this profession called?

   ----------------------------------------------------------------

   ----------------------------------------------------------------

2. What would the world be like if no one did this job?

   ----------------------------------------------------------------

   ----------------------------------------------------------------

   ----------------------------------------------------------------

3. What is a person with this job expected to accomplish?

   ----------------------------------------------------------------

   ----------------------------------------------------------------

   ----------------------------------------------------------------

4. Could you be good at this job? _____ Why?

   ----------------------------------------------------------------

   ----------------------------------------------------------------

   ----------------------------------------------------------------

5. What kind of education, ability, training and experience does a person need to do this job well?

   ----------------------------------------------------------------

   ----------------------------------------------------------------

   ----------------------------------------------------------------

6. How much money can a person earn when they do this job as a profession?

   ----------------------------------------------------------------

7. How much time does this job require?

   ----------------------------------------------------------------

8. Do you know someone with this job?

   ----------------------------------------------------------------

9. On a scale from one to ten, rate this job. 1 2 3 4 5 6 7 8 9 10

10. What is the best thing about this job and the worst thing about this job?

    ----------------------------------------------------------------

    ----------------------------------------------------------------

    ----------------------------------------------------------------

    ----------------------------------------------------------------

    ----------------------------------------------------------------

    ----------------------------------------------------------------

# THINKING QUESTIONS

1. What is this profession called?

   ------------------------------------------------

   ------------------------------------------------

2. What would the world be like if no one did this job?

   ------------------------------------------------

   ------------------------------------------------

   ------------------------------------------------

3. What is a person with this job expected to accomplish?

   ------------------------------------------------

   ------------------------------------------------

   ------------------------------------------------

4. Could you be good at this job? _____ Why?

   ------------------------------------------------

   ------------------------------------------------

   ------------------------------------------------

5. What kind of education, ability, training and experience does a person need to do this job well?

   ------------------------------------------------

   ------------------------------------------------

   ------------------------------------------------

6. How much money can a person earn when they do this job as a profession?

   ------------------------------------------------

7. How much time does this job require?

   ------------------------------------------------

8. Do you know someone with this job?

   ------------------------------------------------

9. On a scale from one to ten, rate this job. 1 2 3 4 5 6 7 8 9 10

10. What is the best thing about this job and the worst thing about this job?

    ------------------------------------------------

    ------------------------------------------------

    ------------------------------------------------

    ------------------------------------------------

    ------------------------------------------------

    ------------------------------------------------

# THINKING QUESTIONS

1. What is this profession called?

   ----------------------------------------------------------------

   ----------------------------------------------------------------

2. What would the world be like if no one did this job?

   ----------------------------------------------------------------

   ----------------------------------------------------------------

   ----------------------------------------------------------------

3. What is a person with this job expected to accomplish?

   ----------------------------------------------------------------

   ----------------------------------------------------------------

   ----------------------------------------------------------------

4. Could you be good at this job? _____ Why?

   ----------------------------------------------------------------

   ----------------------------------------------------------------

   ----------------------------------------------------------------

5. What kind of education, ability, training and experience does a person need to do this job well?

   ----------------------------------------------------------------

   ----------------------------------------------------------------

   ----------------------------------------------------------------

6. How much money can a person earn when they do this job as a profession?

   ----------------------------------------------------------------

7. How much time does this job require?

   ----------------------------------------------------------------

8. Do you know someone with this job?

   ----------------------------------------------------------------

9. On a scale from one to ten, rate this job. 1 2 3 4 5 6 7 8 9 10

10. What is the best thing about this job and the worst thing about this job?

    ----------------------------------------------------------------

    ----------------------------------------------------------------

    ----------------------------------------------------------------

    ----------------------------------------------------------------

    ----------------------------------------------------------------

    ----------------------------------------------------------------

# THINKING QUESTIONS

1.  What is this profession called?

    _____

    _____

2.  What would the world be like if no one did this job?

    _____

    _____

    _____

3.  What is a person with this job expected to accomplish?

    _____

    _____

    _____

4.  Could you be good at this job? _____ Why?

    _____

    _____

    _____

5.  What kind of education, ability, training and experience does a person need to do this job well?

    _____

    _____

    _____

6.  How much money can a person earn when they do this job as a profession?

    _____

7.  How much time does this job require?

    _____

8.  Do you know someone with this job?

    _____

9.  On a scale from one to ten, rate this job. 1 2 3 4 5 6 7 8 9 10

10. What is the best thing about this job and the worst thing about this job?

    _____

    _____

    _____

    _____

    _____

# THINKING QUESTIONS

1.  What is this profession called?

    ---------------------------------------------------------------

2.  What would the world be like if no one did this job?

    ---------------------------------------------------------------

    ---------------------------------------------------------------

3.  What is a person with this job expected to accomplish?

    ---------------------------------------------------------------

    ---------------------------------------------------------------

    ---------------------------------------------------------------

4.  Could you be good at this job? _____ Why?

    ---------------------------------------------------------------

    ---------------------------------------------------------------

    ---------------------------------------------------------------

5.  What kind of education, ability, training and experience does a person need to do this job well?

    ---------------------------------------------------------------

    ---------------------------------------------------------------

    ---------------------------------------------------------------

6.  How much money can a person earn when they do this job as a profession?

    ---------------------------------------------------------------

7.  How much time does this job require?

    ---------------------------------------------------------------

8.  Do you know someone with this job?

    ---------------------------------------------------------------

9.  On a scale from one to ten, rate this job. 1 2 3 4 5 6 7 8 9 10

10. What is the best thing about this job and the worst thing about this job?

    ---------------------------------------------------------------

    ---------------------------------------------------------------

    ---------------------------------------------------------------

    ---------------------------------------------------------------

    ---------------------------------------------------------------

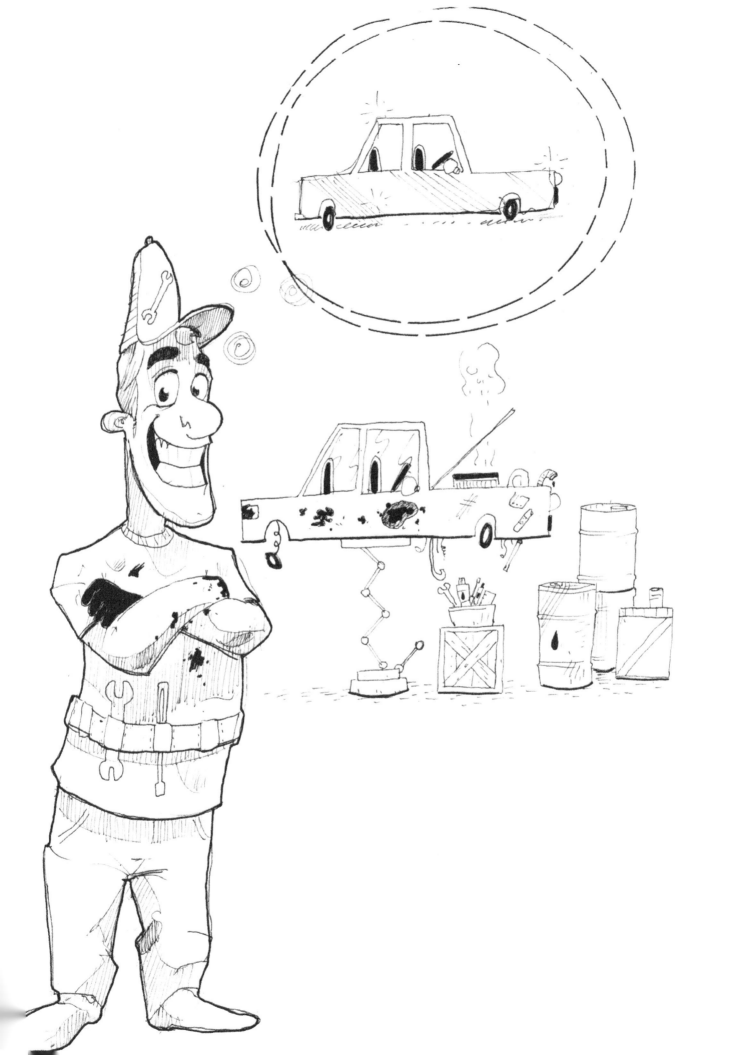

# THINKING QUESTIONS

1.  What is this profession called?

    _____

    _____

2.  What would the world be like if no one did this job?

    _____

    _____

    _____

3.  What is a person with this job expected to accomplish?

    _____

    _____

    _____

4.  Could you be good at this job? _____ Why?

    _____

    _____

    _____

5.  What kind of education, ability, training and experience does a person need to do this job well?

    _____

    _____

    _____

6.  How much money can a person earn when they do this job as a profession?

    _____

7.  How much time does this job require?

    _____

8.  Do you know someone with this job?

    _____

9.  On a scale from one to ten, rate this job. 1 2 3 4 5 6 7 8 9 10

10. What is the best thing about this job and the worst thing about this job?

    _____

    _____

    _____

    _____

    _____

    _____

# THINKING QUESTIONS

1. What is this profession called?

   ------------------------------------------------

   ------------------------------------------------

2. What would the world be like if no one did this job?

   ------------------------------------------------

   ------------------------------------------------

   ------------------------------------------------

3. What is a person with this job expected to accomplish?

   ------------------------------------------------

   ------------------------------------------------

   ------------------------------------------------

4. Could you be good at this job? _____ Why?

   ------------------------------------------------

   ------------------------------------------------

   ------------------------------------------------

5. What kind of education, ability, training and experience does a person need to do this job well?

   ------------------------------------------------

   ------------------------------------------------

   ------------------------------------------------

6. How much money can a person earn when they do this job as a profession?

   ------------------------------------------------

7. How much time does this job require?

   ------------------------------------------------

8. Do you know someone with this job?

   ------------------------------------------------

9. On a scale from one to ten, rate this job. 1 2 3 4 5 6 7 8 9 10

10. What is the best thing about this job and the worst thing about this job?

    ------------------------------------------------

    ------------------------------------------------

    ------------------------------------------------

    ------------------------------------------------

    ------------------------------------------------

    ------------------------------------------------

# THINKING QUESTIONS

1. What is this profession called?

   _____

   _____

2. What would the world be like if no one did this job?

   _____

   _____

   _____

3. What is a person with this job expected to accomplish?

   _____

   _____

   _____

4. Could you be good at this job? _____ Why?

   _____

   _____

   _____

5. What kind of education, ability, training and experience does a person need to do this job well?

   _____

   _____

   _____

6. How much money can a person earn when they do this job as a profession?

   _____

7. How much time does this job require?

   _____

8. Do you know someone with this job?

   _____

9. On a scale from one to ten, rate this job. 1 2 3 4 5 6 7 8 9 10

10. What is the best thing about this job and the worst thing about this job?

   _____

   _____

   _____

   _____

   _____

   _____

# THINKING QUESTIONS

1. What is this profession called?

   ------------------------------------------------------------

   ------------------------------------------------------------

2. What would the world be like if no one did this job?

   ------------------------------------------------------------

   ------------------------------------------------------------

   ------------------------------------------------------------

3. What is a person with this job expected to accomplish?

   ------------------------------------------------------------

   ------------------------------------------------------------

   ------------------------------------------------------------

4. Could you be good at this job? _____ Why?

   ------------------------------------------------------------

   ------------------------------------------------------------

   ------------------------------------------------------------

5. What kind of education, ability, training and experience does a person need to do this job well?

   ------------------------------------------------------------

   ------------------------------------------------------------

   ------------------------------------------------------------

6. How much money can a person earn when they do this job as a profession?

   ------------------------------------------------------------

7. How much time does this job require?

   ------------------------------------------------------------

8. Do you know someone with this job?

   ------------------------------------------------------------

9. On a scale from one to ten, rate this job. 1 2 3 4 5 6 7 8 9 10

10. What is the best thing about this job and the worst thing about this job?

    ------------------------------------------------------------

    ------------------------------------------------------------

    ------------------------------------------------------------

    ------------------------------------------------------------

    ------------------------------------------------------------

# THINKING QUESTIONS

1. What is this profession called?

   _____

   _____

2. What would the world be like if no one did this job?

   _____

   _____

   _____

3. What is a person with this job expected to accomplish?

   _____

   _____

   _____

4. Could you be good at this job? _____ Why?

   _____

   _____

   _____

5. What kind of education, ability, training and experience does a person need to do this job well?

   _____

   _____

   _____

6. How much money can a person earn when they do this job as a profession?

   _____

7. How much time does this job require?

   _____

8. Do you know someone with this job?

   _____

9. On a scale from one to ten, rate this job. 1 2 3 4 5 6 7 8 9 10

10. What is the best thing about this job and the worst thing about this job?

   _____

   _____

   _____

   _____

   _____

   _____

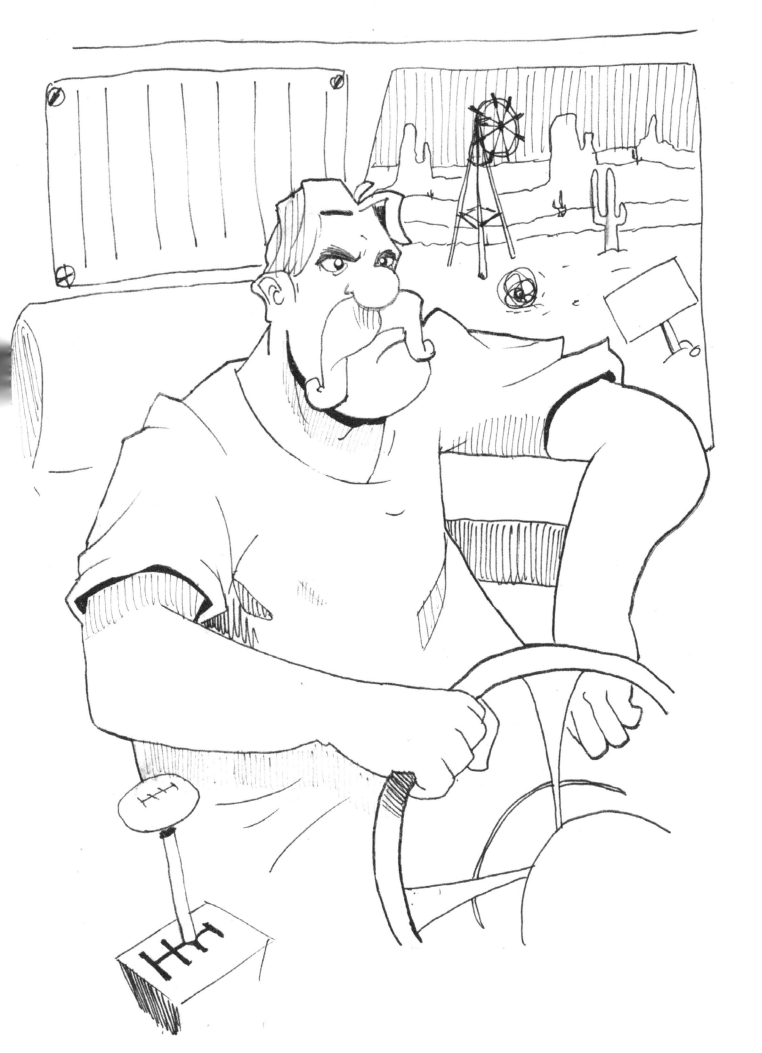

# THINKING QUESTIONS

1.  What is this profession called?

    ------------------------------------------------

    ------------------------------------------------

2.  What would the world be like if no one did this job?

    ------------------------------------------------

    ------------------------------------------------

    ------------------------------------------------

3.  What is a person with this job expected to accomplish?

    ------------------------------------------------

    ------------------------------------------------

    ------------------------------------------------

4.  Could you be good at this job? _____ Why?

    ------------------------------------------------

    ------------------------------------------------

    ------------------------------------------------

5.  What kind of education, ability, training and experience does a person need to do this job well?

    ------------------------------------------------

    ------------------------------------------------

    ------------------------------------------------

6.  How much money can a person earn when they do this job as a profession?

    ------------------------------------------------

7.  How much time does this job require?

    ------------------------------------------------

8.  Do you know someone with this job?

    ------------------------------------------------

9.  On a scale from one to ten, rate this job. 1 2 3 4 5 6 7 8 9 10

10. What is the best thing about this job and the worst thing about this job?

    ------------------------------------------------

    ------------------------------------------------

    ------------------------------------------------

    ------------------------------------------------

    ------------------------------------------------

    ------------------------------------------------

# THINKING QUESTIONS

1. What is this profession called?

   ------------------------------------------------

   ------------------------------------------------

2. What would the world be like if no one did this job?

   ------------------------------------------------

   ------------------------------------------------

   ------------------------------------------------

3. What is a person with this job expected to accomplish?

   ------------------------------------------------

   ------------------------------------------------

   ------------------------------------------------

4. Could you be good at this job? _____ Why?

   ------------------------------------------------

   ------------------------------------------------

   ------------------------------------------------

5. What kind of education, ability, training and experience does a person need to do this job well?

   ------------------------------------------------

   ------------------------------------------------

   ------------------------------------------------

6. How much money can a person earn when they do this job as a profession?

   ------------------------------------------------

7. How much time does this job require?

   ------------------------------------------------

8. Do you know someone with this job?

   ------------------------------------------------

9. On a scale from one to ten, rate this job. 1 2 3 4 5 6 7 8 9 10
10. What is the best thing about this job and the worst thing about this job?

    ------------------------------------------------

    ------------------------------------------------

    ------------------------------------------------

    ------------------------------------------------

    ------------------------------------------------

# THINKING QUESTIONS

1.  What is this profession called?

    -----------------------------------------------------------
    -----------------------------------------------------------

2.  What would the world be like if no one did this job?

    -----------------------------------------------------------
    -----------------------------------------------------------
    -----------------------------------------------------------

3.  What is a person with this job expected to accomplish?

    -----------------------------------------------------------
    -----------------------------------------------------------
    -----------------------------------------------------------

4.  Could you be good at this job? _____ Why?

    -----------------------------------------------------------
    -----------------------------------------------------------
    -----------------------------------------------------------

5.  What kind of education, ability, training and experience does a person need to do this job well?

    -----------------------------------------------------------
    -----------------------------------------------------------
    -----------------------------------------------------------

6.  How much money can a person earn when they do this job as a profession?

    -----------------------------------------------------------

7.  How much time does this job require?

    -----------------------------------------------------------

8.  Do you know someone with this job?

    -----------------------------------------------------------

9.  On a scale from one to ten, rate this job. 1 2 3 4 5 6 7 8 9 10

10. What is the best thing about this job and the worst thing about this job?

    -----------------------------------------------------------
    -----------------------------------------------------------
    -----------------------------------------------------------
    -----------------------------------------------------------
    -----------------------------------------------------------

# THINKING QUESTIONS

1. What is this profession called?

   -----------------------------------------------
   -----------------------------------------------

2. What would the world be like if no one did this job?

   -----------------------------------------------
   -----------------------------------------------
   -----------------------------------------------

3. What is a person with this job expected to accomplish?

   -----------------------------------------------
   -----------------------------------------------
   -----------------------------------------------

4. Could you be good at this job? _____ Why?

   -----------------------------------------------
   -----------------------------------------------
   -----------------------------------------------

5. What kind of education, ability, training and experience does a person need to do this job well?

   -----------------------------------------------
   -----------------------------------------------
   -----------------------------------------------

6. How much money can a person earn when they do this job as a profession?

   -----------------------------------------------

7. How much time does this job require?

   -----------------------------------------------

8. Do you know someone with this job?

   -----------------------------------------------

9. On a scale from one to ten, rate this job. 1 2 3 4 5 6 7 8 9 10

10. What is the best thing about this job and the worst thing about this job?

   -----------------------------------------------
   -----------------------------------------------
   -----------------------------------------------
   -----------------------------------------------
   -----------------------------------------------
   -----------------------------------------------

174

# THINKING QUESTIONS

1. What is this profession called?

   ---------------------------------------------------------------

   ---------------------------------------------------------------

2. What would the world be like if no one did this job?

   ---------------------------------------------------------------

   ---------------------------------------------------------------

   ---------------------------------------------------------------

3. What is a person with this job expected to accomplish?

   ---------------------------------------------------------------

   ---------------------------------------------------------------

   ---------------------------------------------------------------

4. Could you be good at this job? _____ Why?

   ---------------------------------------------------------------

   ---------------------------------------------------------------

   ---------------------------------------------------------------

5. What kind of education, ability, training and experience does a person need to do this job well?

   ---------------------------------------------------------------

   ---------------------------------------------------------------

   ---------------------------------------------------------------

6. How much money can a person earn when they do this job as a profession?

   ---------------------------------------------------------------

7. How much time does this job require?

   ---------------------------------------------------------------

8. Do you know someone with this job?

   ---------------------------------------------------------------

9. On a scale from one to ten, rate this job. 1 2 3 4 5 6 7 8 9 10

10. What is the best thing about this job and the worst thing about this job?

   ---------------------------------------------------------------

   ---------------------------------------------------------------

   ---------------------------------------------------------------

   ---------------------------------------------------------------

   ---------------------------------------------------------------

# THINKING QUESTIONS

1. What is this profession called?

   ------------------------------------------------

   ------------------------------------------------

2. What would the world be like if no one did this job?

   ------------------------------------------------

   ------------------------------------------------

   ------------------------------------------------

3. What is a person with this job expected to accomplish?

   ------------------------------------------------

   ------------------------------------------------

   ------------------------------------------------

4. Could you be good at this job? _____ Why?

   ------------------------------------------------

   ------------------------------------------------

   ------------------------------------------------

5. What kind of education, ability, training and experience does a person need to do this job well?

   ------------------------------------------------

   ------------------------------------------------

   ------------------------------------------------

6. How much money can a person earn when they do this job as a profession?

   ------------------------------------------------

7. How much time does this job require?

   ------------------------------------------------

8. Do you know someone with this job?

   ------------------------------------------------

9. On a scale from one to ten, rate this job. 1 2 3 4 5 6 7 8 9 10

10. What is the best thing about this job and the worst thing about this job?

    ------------------------------------------------

    ------------------------------------------------

    ------------------------------------------------

    ------------------------------------------------

    ------------------------------------------------

    ------------------------------------------------

# THINKING QUESTIONS

1. What is this profession called?

   ------------------------------------------------

   ------------------------------------------------

2. What would the world be like if no one did this job?

   ------------------------------------------------

   ------------------------------------------------

   ------------------------------------------------

3. What is a person with this job expected to accomplish?

   ------------------------------------------------

   ------------------------------------------------

   ------------------------------------------------

4. Could you be good at this job? _____ Why?

   ------------------------------------------------

   ------------------------------------------------

   ------------------------------------------------

5. What kind of education, ability, training and experience does a person need to do this job well?

   ------------------------------------------------

   ------------------------------------------------

   ------------------------------------------------

6. How much money can a person earn when they do this job as a profession?

   ------------------------------------------------

7. How much time does this job require?

   ------------------------------------------------

8. Do you know someone with this job?

   ------------------------------------------------

9. On a scale from one to ten, rate this job. 1 2 3 4 5 6 7 8 9 10

10. What is the best thing about this job and the worst thing about this job?

    ------------------------------------------------

    ------------------------------------------------

    ------------------------------------------------

    ------------------------------------------------

    ------------------------------------------------

    ------------------------------------------------

# THINKING QUESTIONS

1. What is this profession called?

   -------------------------------------------------

   -------------------------------------------------

2. What would the world be like if no one did this job?

   -------------------------------------------------

   -------------------------------------------------

   -------------------------------------------------

3. What is a person with this job expected to accomplish?

   -------------------------------------------------

   -------------------------------------------------

   -------------------------------------------------

4. Could you be good at this job? _____ Why?

   -------------------------------------------------

   -------------------------------------------------

   -------------------------------------------------

5. What kind of education, ability, training and experience does a person need to do this job well?

   -------------------------------------------------

   -------------------------------------------------

   -------------------------------------------------

6. How much money can a person earn when they do this job as a profession?

   -------------------------------------------------

7. How much time does this job require?

   -------------------------------------------------

8. Do you know someone with this job?

   -------------------------------------------------

9. On a scale from one to ten, rate this job. 1 2 3 4 5 6 7 8 9 10

10. What is the best thing about this job and the worst thing about this job?

    -------------------------------------------------

    -------------------------------------------------

    -------------------------------------------------

    -------------------------------------------------

    -------------------------------------------------

    -------------------------------------------------

# THINKING QUESTIONS

1. What is this profession called?

   ----------------------------------------

   ----------------------------------------

2. What would the world be like if no one did this job?

   ----------------------------------------

   ----------------------------------------

   ----------------------------------------

3. What is a person with this job expected to accomplish?

   ----------------------------------------

   ----------------------------------------

   ----------------------------------------

4. Could you be good at this job? _____ Why?

   ----------------------------------------

   ----------------------------------------

   ----------------------------------------

5. What kind of education, ability, training and experience does a person need to do this job well?

   ----------------------------------------

   ----------------------------------------

   ----------------------------------------

6. How much money can a person earn when they do this job as a profession?

   ----------------------------------------

7. How much time does this job require?

   ----------------------------------------

8. Do you know someone with this job?

   ----------------------------------------

9. On a scale from one to ten, rate this job. 1 2 3 4 5 6 7 8 9 10

10. What is the best thing about this job and the worst thing about this job?

    ----------------------------------------

    ----------------------------------------

    ----------------------------------------

    ----------------------------------------

    ----------------------------------------

    ----------------------------------------

# THINKING QUESTIONS

1. What is this profession called?

   ----------------------------------------

   ----------------------------------------

2. What would the world be like if no one did this job?

   ----------------------------------------

   ----------------------------------------

   ----------------------------------------

3. What is a person with this job expected to accomplish?

   ----------------------------------------

   ----------------------------------------

   ----------------------------------------

4. Could you be good at this job? _____ Why?

   ----------------------------------------

   ----------------------------------------

   ----------------------------------------

5. What kind of education, ability, training and experience does a person need to do this job well?

   ----------------------------------------

   ----------------------------------------

   ----------------------------------------

6. How much money can a person earn when they do this job as a profession?

   ----------------------------------------

7. How much time does this job require?

   ----------------------------------------

8. Do you know someone with this job?

   ----------------------------------------

9. On a scale from one to ten, rate this job. 1 2 3 4 5 6 7 8 9 10
10. What is the best thing about this job and the worst thing about this job?

   ----------------------------------------

   ----------------------------------------

   ----------------------------------------

   ----------------------------------------

   ----------------------------------------

   ----------------------------------------

# THINKING QUESTIONS

1. What is this profession called?

   -------------------------------------------------

   -------------------------------------------------

2. What would the world be like if no one did this job?

   -------------------------------------------------

   -------------------------------------------------

   -------------------------------------------------

3. What is a person with this job expected to accomplish?

   -------------------------------------------------

   -------------------------------------------------

   -------------------------------------------------

4. Could you be good at this job? _____ Why?

   -------------------------------------------------

   -------------------------------------------------

   -------------------------------------------------

5. What kind of education, ability, training and experience does a person need to do this job well?

   -------------------------------------------------

   -------------------------------------------------

   -------------------------------------------------

6. How much money can a person earn when they do this job as a profession?

   -------------------------------------------------

7. How much time does this job require?

   -------------------------------------------------

8. Do you know someone with this job?

   -------------------------------------------------

9. On a scale from one to ten, rate this job. 1 2 3 4 5 6 7 8 9 10

10. What is the best thing about this job and the worst thing about this job?

   -------------------------------------------------

   -------------------------------------------------

   -------------------------------------------------

   -------------------------------------------------

   -------------------------------------------------

   -------------------------------------------------

# THINKING QUESTIONS

1. What is this profession called?

   _____
   _____

2. What would the world be like if no one did this job?

   _____
   _____
   _____

3. What is a person with this job expected to accomplish?

   _____
   _____
   _____

4. Could you be good at this job? _____ Why?

   _____
   _____
   _____

5. What kind of education, ability, training and experience does a person need to do this job well?

   _____
   _____
   _____

6. How much money can a person earn when they do this job as a profession?

   _____

7. How much time does this job require?

   _____

8. Do you know someone with this job?

   _____

9. On a scale from one to ten, rate this job. 1 2 3 4 5 6 7 8 9 10

10. What is the best thing about this job and the worst thing about this job?

   _____
   _____
   _____
   _____
   _____
   _____

# THINKING QUESTIONS

1. What is this profession called?

   ----------------------------------------

   ----------------------------------------

2. What would the world be like if no one did this job?

   ----------------------------------------

   ----------------------------------------

   ----------------------------------------

3. What is a person with this job expected to accomplish?

   ----------------------------------------

   ----------------------------------------

   ----------------------------------------

4. Could you be good at this job? _____ Why?

   ----------------------------------------

   ----------------------------------------

   ----------------------------------------

5. What kind of education, ability, training and experience does a person need to do this job well?

   ----------------------------------------

   ----------------------------------------

   ----------------------------------------

6. How much money can a person earn when they do this job as a profession?

   ----------------------------------------

7. How much time does this job require?

   ----------------------------------------

8. Do you know someone with this job?

   ----------------------------------------

9. On a scale from one to ten, rate this job. 1 2 3 4 5 6 7 8 9 10

10. What is the best thing about this job and the worst thing about this job?

   ----------------------------------------

   ----------------------------------------

   ----------------------------------------

   ----------------------------------------

   ----------------------------------------

   ----------------------------------------

# THINKING QUESTIONS

1. What is this profession called?

   ------------------------------------------------

   ------------------------------------------------

2. What would the world be like if no one did this job?

   ------------------------------------------------

   ------------------------------------------------

   ------------------------------------------------

3. What is a person with this job expected to accomplish?

   ------------------------------------------------

   ------------------------------------------------

   ------------------------------------------------

4. Could you be good at this job? _____ Why?

   ------------------------------------------------

   ------------------------------------------------

   ------------------------------------------------

5. What kind of education, ability, training and experience does a person need to do this job well?

   ------------------------------------------------

   ------------------------------------------------

   ------------------------------------------------

6. How much money can a person earn when they do this job as a profession?

   ------------------------------------------------

7. How much time does this job require?

   ------------------------------------------------

8. Do you know someone with this job?

   ------------------------------------------------

9. On a scale from one to ten, rate this job. 1 2 3 4 5 6 7 8 9 10

10. What is the best thing about this job and the worst thing about this job?

    ------------------------------------------------

    ------------------------------------------------

    ------------------------------------------------

    ------------------------------------------------

    ------------------------------------------------

    ------------------------------------------------

# THINKING QUESTIONS

1. What is this profession called?

   -----------------------------------------------------------------

   -----------------------------------------------------------------

2. What would the world be like if no one did this job?

   -----------------------------------------------------------------

   -----------------------------------------------------------------

   -----------------------------------------------------------------

3. What is a person with this job expected to accomplish?

   -----------------------------------------------------------------

   -----------------------------------------------------------------

   -----------------------------------------------------------------

4. Could you be good at this job? _____ Why?

   -----------------------------------------------------------------

   -----------------------------------------------------------------

   -----------------------------------------------------------------

5. What kind of education, ability, training and experience does a
   person need to do this job well?

   -----------------------------------------------------------------

   -----------------------------------------------------------------

   -----------------------------------------------------------------

6. How much money can a person earn when they do this job as a
   profession?

   -----------------------------------------------------------------

7. How much time does this job require?

   -----------------------------------------------------------------

8. Do you know someone with this job?

   -----------------------------------------------------------------

9. On a scale from one to ten, rate this job. 1 2 3 4 5 6 7 8 9 10
10. What is the best thing about this job and the worst thing about this
    job?

   -----------------------------------------------------------------

   -----------------------------------------------------------------

   -----------------------------------------------------------------

   -----------------------------------------------------------------

   -----------------------------------------------------------------

   -----------------------------------------------------------------

# HOW TO MAKE MONEY

# YOUR GUIDE

## FOR CHOOSING AND PURSUING YOUR CAREER.

# PLANS AND GOALS (HAVE THEY CHANGED?)

What do you want to be doing two years from now?

YEAR: _____ My Age:_____

------------------------------------------------

------------------------------------------------

------------------------------------------------

------------------------------------------------

------------------------------------------------

What do you want to be doing 15 years from now?

YEAR:_____ My Age:_____

------------------------------------------------

------------------------------------------------

------------------------------------------------

------------------------------------------------

------------------------------------------------

------------------------------------------------

What do your need to LEARN or CHANGE in your life now so you can reach your future goals?

------------------------------------------------

------------------------------------------------

------------------------------------------------

------------------------------------------------

------------------------------------------------

------------------------------------------------

**2. Learn everything you can about those ten jobs. Read books, watch videos and talk to people who do the jobs that interest you.**

## BOOK LIST:

_____

_____

_____

_____

_____

_____

_____

_____

_____

_____

_____

_____

# Profession #1

------------------------------------

------------------------------------

------------------------------------

------------------------------------

------------------------------------

------------------------------------

------------------------------------

------------------------------------

------------------------------------

------------------------------------

------------------------------------

------------------------------------

------------------------------------

------------------------------------

------------------------------------

------------------------------------

# Profession #2

------------------------------

------------------------------

------------------------------

------------------------------

------------------------------

------------------------------

------------------------------

------------------------------

------------------------------

------------------------------

------------------------------

------------------------------

------------------------------

------------------------------

# Profession #3

------------------------------

-------------------------------------

-------------------------------------

-------------------------------------

-------------------------------------

-------------------------------------

-------------------------------------

-------------------------------------

-------------------------------------

-------------------------------------

-------------------------------------

-------------------------------------

-------------------------------------

-------------------------------------

----------------- Profession #3 -----------

# Profession #4

_____

_____

_____

_____

_____

_____

_____

_____

_____

_____

_____

_____

_____

_____

_____

_____ Profession #4 _____

# Profession #5

_____

_____

_____

_____

_____

_____

_____

_____

_____

_____

_____

_____

_____

_____

_____

_____

_____

_____

# Profession #6

_____

_____

_____

_____

_____

_____

_____

_____

_____

_____

_____

_____

_____

_____

_____

_____Profession #6_____

# Profession #7

----------------------------------------

----------------------------------------

----------------------------------------

----------------------------------------

----------------------------------------

----------------------------------------

----------------------------------------

----------------------------------------

----------------------------------------

----------------------------------------

----------------------------------------

----------------------------------------

----------------------------------------

----------------------------------------

----------------------------------------

----------------------------------------

-------------------- Profession #7 --------------------

# Profession #8

_____

_____

_____

_____

_____

_____

_____

_____

_____

_____

_____

_____

_____

_____

_____

_____

# Profession #9

----------------------------

- - - - - - - - - - - - - - - - - - - - - - - - - - - - - -

- - - - - - - - - - - - - - - - - - - - - - - - - - - - - -

- - - - - - - - - - - - - - - - - - - - - - - - - - - - - -

- - - - - - - - - - - - - - - - - - - - - - - - - - - - - -

- - - - - - - - - - - - - - - - - - - - - - - - - - - - - -

- - - - - - - - - - - - - - - - - - - - - - - - - - - - - -

- - - - - - - - - - - - - - - - - - - - - - - - - - - - - -

- - - - - - - - - - - - - - - - - - - - - - - - - - - - - -

- - - - - - - - - - - - - - - - - - - - - - - - - - - - - -

- - - - - - - - - - - - - - - - - - - - - - - - - - - - - -

- - - - - - - - - - - - - - - - - - - - - - - - - - - - - -

- - - - - - - - - - - - - - - - - - - - - - - - - - - - - -

- - - - - - - - - - - - - - - - - - - - - - - - - - - - - -

- - - - - - - - - - - - - - - - - - - - - - - - - - - - - -

- - - - - - - - - - - - - - - - - - - - - - - - - - - - - -

# Profession #10

----------------------------------

--------------------------------------

--------------------------------------

--------------------------------------

--------------------------------------

--------------------------------------

--------------------------------------

--------------------------------------

--------------------------------------

--------------------------------------

--------------------------------------

--------------------------------------

--------------------------------------

--------------------------------------

--------------------------------------

--------------------------Profession #10----------------

# Choose FOUR Professions to Research

3. When you learn everything you can about those jobs, narrow your list down to four occupations that you might pursue.

Choose two jobs that require higher education and two jobs that you can start doing right away.

1. _____

2. _____

3. _____

4. _____

# Interview a Professional #1

_____

_____

_____

_____

_____

_____

_____

_____

_____

_____

_____

_____

_____

_____Interview a Professional #1_____

# Interview a Professional #2

_____

_____

_____

_____

_____

_____

_____

_____

_____

_____

_____

_____

_____

_____

_____

_____

# Interview a Professional #3

_____

---------------------------------------

---------------------------------------

---------------------------------------

---------------------------------------

---------------------------------------

---------------------------------------

---------------------------------------

---------------------------------------

---------------------------------------

---------------------------------------

---------------------------------------

---------------------------------------

---------------------------------------

---------------------------------------

# Interview a Professional #4

-------------------------------

- - - - - - - - - - - - - - - - - - - - - - - - - - - - - -

- - - - - - - - - - - - - - - - - - - - - - - - - - - - - -

- - - - - - - - - - - - - - - - - - - - - - - - - - - - - -

- - - - - - - - - - - - - - - - - - - - - - - - - - - - - -

- - - - - - - - - - - - - - - - - - - - - - - - - - - - - -

- - - - - - - - - - - - - - - - - - - - - - - - - - - - - -

- - - - - - - - - - - - - - - - - - - - - - - - - - - - - -

- - - - - - - - - - - - - - - - - - - - - - - - - - - - - -

- - - - - - - - - - - - - - - - - - - - - - - - - - - - - -

- - - - - - - - - - - - - - - - - - - - - - - - - - - - - -

- - - - - - - - - - - - - - - - - - - - - - - - - - - - - -

- - - - - - - - - - - - - - - - - - - - - - - - - - - - - -

- - - - - - - - - - - - - - - - - - - - - - - - - - - - - -

- - - - - - - - - - - - - - - - - - - - - - - - - - - - - -

- - - - - - - - - - - - - - - - - Interview a Professional #4 - - - - - - -

5. Train yourself to become an expert
about your TWO favorite occupations!
Choose one that requires higher education
and one you can start doing now!

How I will earn Money NOW:

---------------------------------------------------

---------------------------------------------------

---------------------------------------------------

---------------------------------------------------

---------------------------------------------------

---------------------------------------------------

How I will earn Money in the Future:

---------------------------------------------------

---------------------------------------------------

---------------------------------------------------

---------------------------------------------------

---------------------------------------------------

---------------------------------------------------

---------------------------------------------------

# 6. Volunteer or intern as an assistant to someone with your favorite jobs.

## NOTES:

_____

_____

_____

_____

_____

_____

_____

_____

_____

_____

_____

_____

_____

_____

_____

_____

# 7. Acquire the education, experience, abilities and skills to be the best at your chosen professions.

## NOTES:

-------------------------------------------------

-------------------------------------------------

-------------------------------------------------

-------------------------------------------------

-------------------------------------------------

-------------------------------------------------

-------------------------------------------------

-------------------------------------------------

-------------------------------------------------

-------------------------------------------------

-------------------------------------------------

-------------------------------------------------

-------------------------------------------------

-------------------------------------------------

-------7. Acquire the education, experience, abilities-----

-----and skills to be the best at your chosen professions.----

# 8. Find out how to do your job so well that people will pay you well to do it.

## NOTES:

-------------------------------------------------------

-------------------------------------------------------

-------------------------------------------------------

-------------------------------------------------------

-------------------------------------------------------

-------------------------------------------------------

-------------------------------------------------------

-------------------------------------------------------

-------------------------------------------------------

-------------------------------------------------------

-------------------------------------------------------

-------------------------------------------------------

-------------------------------------------------------

-------------------------------------------------------

-------------------------------------------------------

-------------------------------------------------------

# 9. Write down all the character traits and virtues that are essential in your work and social relationships.

-------------------------------------------------------

-------------------------------------------------------

-------------------------------------------------------

-------------------------------------------------------

-------------------------------------------------------

-------------------------------------------------------

-------------------------------------------------------

-------------------------------------------------------

-------------------------------------------------------

-------------------------------------------------------

-------------------------------------------------------

-------------------------------------------------------

-------------------------------------------------------

-------------------------------------------------------

---------9. Write down all the character traits---------

-------------------------------------------------------

# PLANS AND GOALS (HAVE THEY CHANGED?)

What do you want to be doing two years from now?

YEAR: _____ My Age:_____

_____

_____

_____

_____

_____

What do you want to be doing 15 years from now?

YEAR:_____ My Age:_____

_____

_____

_____

_____

_____

What do your need to LEARN or CHANGE in your life now so you can reach your future goals?

_____

_____

_____

_____

_____

_____

# 10. Make Plans and Set Goals.

Today: _____

----------------------------------------

----------------------------------------

----------------------------------------

----------------------------------------

----------------------------------------

----------------------------------------

----------------------------------------

----------------------------------------

Tomorrow: _____

----------------------------------------

----------------------------------------

----------------------------------------

----------------------------------------

----------------------------------------

----------------------------------------

----------------------------------------

----------------------------------------

## One Month From Now: _____

----------------------------------------

----------------------------------------

----------------------------------------

----------------------------------------

----------------------------------------

----------------------------------------

----------------------------------------

----------------------------------------

----------------------------------------

## One Year From Now: _____

----------------------------------------

----------------------------------------

----------------------------------------

----------------------------------------

----------------------------------------

----------------------------------------

----------------------------------------

----------------------------------------

----------------------------------------

# Plans and Goals

## 3 Years for Now: _____

---------------------------------------------------------

---------------------------------------------------------

---------------------------------------------------------

---------------------------------------------------------

---------------------------------------------------------

---------------------------------------------------------

---------------------------------------------------------

---------------------------------------------------------

## 5 Years from Now: _____

---------------------------------------------------------

---------------------------------------------------------

---------------------------------------------------------

---------------------------------------------------------

---------------------------------------------------------

---------------------------------------------------------

---------------------------------------------------------

---------------------------------------------------------

10 Years From Now: _____

----------------------------------------

----------------------------------------

----------------------------------------

----------------------------------------

----------------------------------------

----------------------------------------

----------------------------------------

----------------------------------------

----------------------------------------

20 Years From Now: _____

----------------------------------------

----------------------------------------

----------------------------------------

----------------------------------------

----------------------------------------

----------------------------------------

----------------------------------------

----------------------------------------

# Plans and Goals

30 Years for Now: _____

---------------------------------------------------------------

---------------------------------------------------------------

---------------------------------------------------------------

---------------------------------------------------------------

---------------------------------------------------------------

---------------------------------------------------------------

---------------------------------------------------------------

---------------------------------------------------------------

---------------------------------------------------------------

50 Years from Now: _____

---------------------------------------------------------------

---------------------------------------------------------------

---------------------------------------------------------------

---------------------------------------------------------------

---------------------------------------------------------------

---------------------------------------------------------------

---------------------------------------------------------------

# NOTES

# The Thinking Tree Publishing Company, LLC

## Copyright Information

### Contact Us:

The Thinking Tree LLC

617 N. Swope St. Greenfield, IN 46140. United States

317.622.8852 PHONE (Dial +1 outside of the USA) 267.712.7889 FAX

www.DyslexiaGames.com

jbrown@DyslexiaGames.com

Made in the USA
Las Vegas, NV
11 August 2023

75948477R00129